COMMUNAL SOCIETIES IN AMERICA
AN AMS REPRINT SERIES

SHAKERS.

COMPENDIUM

Evans, Frederick W.

Andrew S. Thomas Memorial Library
MORRIS HARVEY COLLEGE, CHARLESTON, W. VA.

AMS PRESS
NEW YORK

289.8
Ev15s

FOURTH EDITION.

SHAKERS.

COMPENDIUM

OF THE

ORIGIN, HISTORY, PRINCIPLES, RULES AND REGULATIONS, GOVERNMENT, AND DOCTRINES

OF THE

UNITED SOCIETY OF BELIEVERS IN CHRIST'S SECOND APPEARING.

WITH BIOGRAPHIES OF

ANN LEE,

WILLIAM LEE, JAS. WHITTAKER, J. HOCKNELL, J. MEACHAM, AND LUCY WRIGHT.

BY F. W. EVANS.

"O my soul, swallow down understanding, and devour wisdom; for thou hast only time to live."—ESDRAS.

NEW LEBANON, N.Y.

1867.

Library of Congress Cataloging in Publication Data

Evans, Frederick William, 1808-1893.
   Shakers: compendium of the origin, history, principles, rules and regulations, government, and doctrines of the United Society of Believers in Christ's Second Appearing. . . .

   (Communal societies in America)
   Reprint of the 1867 ed. (4th ed.) printed by C. Van Benthuysen, Albany.
   Bibliography: p.
   1. Shakers. 2. Shakers—Biography. 3. Lee, Ann, 1736-1784. 4. Lee, William, 1740-1784. 5. Whittaker, James, 1751-1787. 6. Hocknell, John, 1723?-1799. 7. Meacham, Joseph, 1742-1796. 8. Wright, Lucy, 1760-1821. I. Title: Compendium of the origin, history, principles, rules and regulations, government, and doctrines of the United Society of Believers in Christ's Second Appearing.
BX9771.E85   1975   289.8   72-2985
ISBN 0-404-10747-8

Reprinted from an original copy in the collection of the University of Connecticut Library.

From the edition of 1867, New Lebanon, Fourth Edition
First AMS edition published in 1975
Manufactured in the United States of America

AMS PRESS INC.
NEW YORK, N.Y. 10003

TO THE READER.

IN respectful response to the often-expressed desire of the public, to have the information respecting *Shakers* and *Shakerism*, that is now spread through some five or six volumes, concentrated in a Compendium, this work has been prepared by the author and compiler, in union with, and aided by, his Gospel friends.

It being, as stated in all previous publications by the Society, the settled faith of the Church, from the beginning, that *its foundation* was Divine REVELATION; and that the records of past Dispensations, and their revelations, can be understood and interpreted aright *only* by means of a *present living revelation;* we therefore feel ourselves untrammeled by the *letter* of *yesterday*, and write and express our views in accordance with the increasing *light* of *to-day*, as we hope and trust, subject to the dictates of "the Comforter," or "Spirit of Truth," dwelling and abiding in the Church, which is gradually, but surely and safely, leading it into the knowledge of "*all truth.*" For "in Christ are hid," as we fully believe, "all the treasures of wisdom and knowledge."

F. W. EVANS,
CALVIN GREEN, } Committee of Revision.
GILES AVERY.

August, 1858.

INTRODUCTION.

The *United Society of Believers* in Christ's Second Appearing, at this day, stand before the public in a very different attitude from what they have ever done at the time of issuing any of their previous publications.

Many of the most obnoxious features of the Society—such as drew down upon it the opposition and secret or open persecution, particularly of religious professors—are now becoming the popular views of the times, at least of all the progressive minds of the age.

Again. The ignorant or willful misconceptions of what were the actual doctrines, principles, and faith of the Society, are being corrected; and the false judgings of certain discrepancies existing between the profession and practice of the people, are almost entirely removed from the public mind.

It is no longer believed that Ann Lee was a "*witch*," because she was known to possess supernatural powers; or that the Shakers think her to be something more than human—equal to Christ; or that they worship her, etc., etc.

It is now generally known, that we do not condemn the Marriage institution, in its *own order*, and when governed by its *true laws;* but simply hold that it is *not* a *Christian* institution.

The wonderful and almost incredible openings of light and truth pertaining to this and the external spiritual world, and which address themselves almost exclusively to the external man, by sensuous facts and physical demonstrations, and which, in former times and other ages, were suppressed and condemned, as the effect of unlawful communings with the powers of darkness, are now being received with joy and gladness by thousands of persons, as proof of a *telegraphic* communication established between the two worlds; and no more to be disputed or doubted than is the existence of that marvelous submarine *telegraphic cable* that connects the Eastern and Western continents.

In all these advances of the human mind in knowledge relating to the mundane and supermundane planes, we find cause for hope and encouragement that the time is drawing nigh when the interior and truly *spiritual* powers of the souls of our fellow-creatures will be awakened as from a long night of slumber, and when human *hearts* will be touched with the fire of conviction for sin, from the altar of *religious truth*, quickening them into that affection for each other that shall burn up selfishness, and draw them, as with strong cords of love, into communities of brotherhood and sisterhood, not only under a Christian *profession*, but also into a Christian *practice*—a CHRISTIAN CHURCH.

All truth, being primarily of Divine origin, is fit food for human souls when "rightly divided" and properly used. The observation of natural facts and phenomena on the earth plane, and the orderly arrangement of such facts, together with the scientific deduction of general principles therefrom, which can be applied to the use and benefit of mankind, are, in their place and order, right and good.

With such knowledge we have no war; for "we can do nothing against the truth, but for the truth." All truth, when *un*adulterated with human pride and self, is a *unit*. And *true* earthly knowledge, talents, and capacities bear the same relation to the Divine revelation of spiritual good and truth that the vessels which the widow borrowed bore to her cruse of oil. There was no limit to the flow of the precious oil, except the number and size of the vessels that contained it.

It is man's duty in this world to cultivate his natural powers and capacities, solely with reference to the rendering himself the better recipient of the truths of the higher spheres, and of the elements of eternal existence. The Divine revelations of former Dispensations were limited and molded by the knowledge of *this natural* world of the mediums and people of those times.

"Moses was learned in all the wisdom of the Egyptians;" and their ideas of geology and astronomy governed, in a measure, his account of the creation, though written by inspiration; as was also that of the lengthening of the day when the "sun stood still upon the mount Gibeon, and the moon in the valley of Ajalon."

Let us all, then, be diligent to add " to our faith virtue; and to virtue knowledge; and to knowledge temperance; and to temperance patience; and to patience *godliness*, which is profitable unto all things, of the life that now is, and of that which is to come;" and thus we shall abound in that true love to God which results in loving our neighbor as we love ourselves.

CONTENTS.

	PAGE
INTRODUCTION	5
CHAPTER I.—Origin of the Society	11
" II.—Rise, Progress, and Present State of the Society	25
" III.—Qualifications for Membership, and Rules and Regulations	42
" IV.—Characteristics and Doctrines of Jesus Christ	56
" V.—Character of the Primitive Christian Church	65
" VI.—Fall of the Primitive Christian Church	71
" VII.—Rise of the "Two Witnesses"	78
" VIII.—Character of the Church of Christ's Second Appearing	86
" IX.—Mode of Worship	90
" X.—Doctrines of the Church of Christ's Second Appearing—	
PART I.—Mosaic Sabbaths, and Higher and Lower Law	94
" II.—Probation, and Heavens and Hells	98

CONTENTS.

	PAGE
PART III.—God *dual*—Father and Mother..	103
" IV.—Judgment-day, and Confession of Sins	114
" V.—The Bible	118
CHAPTER XI.—Biographies of the Six Founders of the Shaker Society—Ann Lee	120
" XII.—William Lee	156
" XIII.—James Whittaker	160
" XIV.—John Hocknell	181
" XV.—Joseph Meacham and Lucy Wright	183
List of Books published by the Society, and List of the Branches of the Society, with their Locations and Addresses	186, 188

SHAKERS AND SHAKERISM.

CHAPTER I.

ORIGIN OF THE SOCIETY.

1. SHAKERISM is claimed, by its advocates, to be the ultimate, or *second Christian*, *Church*— the *Millennium*.

2. The inquiry naturally arises, What elements produced the Shaker Societies? To meet this, reference must be had to historical facts bearing upon the subject. But let the following proposition be first considered: namely, that at a given part, point, and time of every cycle of human affairs, in all ages, nations, and tribes, there have invariably arisen an order and people analogous (in some measure) to the American *Shakers*. No matter what the name by which history designates

them; they are easily recognized by certain distinguishing marks.

3. China, Persia, India had their ascetics; Rome, her sibyls and vestals; Egypt, her Therapeutics; and Judea, the self-denying Essenes, among whom it is thought Jesus received his education and early training. Speaking of these, Philo says: "In many parts of the earth, such a people exist; for it is fitting that both Greek and Barbarian share in the absolute good." Pliny the Elder says: "The Essenes were a sort of people who lived without women and money."

4. As the lowest types of humanity are those who seek happiness the most exclusively in the indulgence of the baser and animal propensities, so the saints of all times have moved the farthest in the opposite direction. Abstinence from sexual intercourse, from private property, from war, oaths, and the honors of the world, have ever been the chief characteristics of ascetics, in all ages.

5. The principles and maxims of Jesus, as explained and confirmed by his own teaching and practice, and measurably by that of his first twelve

converts and most intimate friends, the Apostles, seem to give countenance to the idea, that some great and important *truths* underlie all these (often) abnormal operations of mind that, from age to age, were struggling for expression and embodiment in human action.

6. The whole of human history is comprised within four large cycles, three of which are already past, and the fourth has commenced. Within these exist an almost infinity of smaller cycles, as was well and beautifully illustrated to the prophet Ezekiel, in a vision of a number of wheels revolving within wheels.

7. Every cycle of human history, whether on a low or high plane, or small or large scale, has its point of highest development: first, of the *physical;* devoted to the supply of the mere animal or bodily wants: second, of the *moral;* which subserves a negative protective influence to the physical: third, of the *intellectual powers;* by which tools and machinery are created (constituting man a tool-making animal), which facilitate and increase the means of physical subsistence, and greatly en-

hance the enjoyment of the moral faculties, on the one hand; and, on the other, they prepare the soul for the opening of its spiritual capacities; by which means an intelligent union and connection is formed and sustained between the visible and invisible earths, or worlds, and their respective inhabitants.

8. All these, combined, form the basis of the final unfoldment of the last and highest property and faculty of the soul, viz., the *religious*. Consequently the quality and abstract truthfulness of the purest form of religion evolved in any given cycle, was determined by the *time of day* in the great year of progress, and the number and plane of the cycle. But, whether higher or lower, it was, in its degree, the witness of the Church of the future—a lively type of *Shakerism*, the ultimate Christian, or *Millennial*, Church, for the redemption of our race.

9. Whenever, in a cycle, the culminating point of Spiritualism has been reached, then the *religious* element has moved thereupon, and finally ultimated itself in a Church, which was emphatically the Church of God of that cycle and period.

10. The flood of Noah was merely the greatest spiritual-physical manifestation of the cycle of that day. The building of the ark was the organization of the religious constructive elements that moved upon the spiritual. In the next great cycle the spiritual elements had, in Egypt, progressed and ripened up in the days of Moses. The ten plagues were ten spiritual-physical manifestations; and Moses came off conqueror, in his contests with the Egyptian magicians (spiritual media), because he was vitalized by the *religious* or controlling element of that order.

11. Under its influence, Moses organized the whole nation of the Hebrews into a highly spiritualized religious body, or Church; the most perfect that had ever been established upon earth, for the simple yet significant reason, that he had been previously fully developed in all the preceding preparatory degrees of the cycle. He "was learned in all the wisdom of the Egyptians, and was mighty in word and deed," having been educated under the auspices of the royal family.

12. The *third* great cycle culminated in Spirit-

ualism, in the days of *Jesus*. That such is the fact, is abundantly proved by the testimony of profane as well as sacred history. Dr. Lightfoot observes: "Judea was so infested with spirits at that time, that thousands of persons were obsessed by them; many of whom Jesus and his disciples released." Josephus, an eye-witness, relates, that sights, sounds, and voices were seen and heard by the whole city of Jerusalem. And, according to the Scriptural records, *dumb animals* were sometimes taken possession of by spirits.

13. Spiritual-physical manifestations attended the whole life of John and Jesus, from their conception to their death. The *religious* elements of that cycle were concentrated in Jesus, as an *individual*. At the day of Pentecost, the same elements concentred, and were organized in the most spiritually endowed body of people, or Church, that any cycle had ever been capable of producing.

14. Jesus and his Apostles continually referred to the next, or *fourth* and *last*, great cycle as the time for "*the restitution of all things*, which God

had spoken by the mouth of all his prophets [in all nations and cycles] since the world began." It was at the spiritual acme of this cycle, that the Christ (whom John saw as a dove appear to Jesus) would come *again*, to some other individual. This *second coming*, the Shakers claim, must of necessity have been to a *woman*, because the race is *female as well as male*.

15. We will endeavor to show, in its right place, from proper historical data, that the *rise* of the *Shaker* Church, or order, has been agreeable to the premises above laid down; as has also the formation of all the Shaker communities.

16. Dr. Adam Clarke says: "Every dispensation of God must begin in some *one individual*, and at some particular time and place." That is correct. A true Church could have originated only by a *new revelation* from God to some *one* person; and then by that person reducing the truths and requirements thereof to practice.

17. Shaker Societies always originate in the *spiritual* part of a cycle. There is, first, a general agitation of the *spiritual* elements; out of that

arises a movement of the *religious* elements in man. This leads to the formation of one or more Shaker Societies, according to the order of the cycle that is revolving. Therefore the Shakers now confidently expect the time has nearly arrived for a further extension of their order.

18. The natural and spiritual worlds are now coming into a state of rapport with each other; and the spiritual faculties in man, which have for a long time been in a state of dormancy, are being aroused and developed very extensively; and soon the religious nature of man will be quickened, and religious revivals will commence on a grander and more effective scale than have ever been witnessed; for they will rest upon the basis of, and spread over the ground prepared by, *Spiritualism*.

19. In the beginning of the eighteenth century, Spiritualism broke out on the continent of Europe, and was followed by most remarkable religious revivals; out of which arose the "French prophets." These were wrought upon in a very extraordinary manner; not only in their minds, but also in their physical systems. They had visions and trances,

and were subject to violent agitations of body. Men and women, and even little children, were so exercised, as that spectators were struck with great wonder and astonishment. Their powerful admonitions and prophetic warnings were heard and received with reverence and awe.

20. They testified that the end of all things drew nigh; and admonished the people to repent, and amend their lives. They gave warning of the near approach of the kingdom of heaven, the "acceptable year of the Lord;" and, in many prophetic messages, declared to the world, that those numerous Scripture prophecies concerning the new heaven and the new earth, the kingdom of the Messiah, the Marriage of the Lamb, the first resurrection, and the New Jerusalem descending from above, were near at hand, and would shortly be accomplished.

21. They also testified, with great power and energy of spirit, against those false systems of religion, and that antichristian dominion, which had borne such extensive sway among mankind; and predicted their certain downfall and destruction.

They declared that, when all these false systems, of human invention, and all the deceitful and abominable works of man, should be pulled down and destroyed, there would be but one Lord, one faith, one heart, and one voice among mankind; and that these things would be wrought by a *spiritual* influence proceeding from living witnesses, who, by the inspiration of the Spirit, should be sent forth as laborers into the harvest field.

22. They continued their prophetic warnings (under much persecution) for several years, over the greater part of Europe. And, in the year 1706, the revival extended to England, where it spread far and wide.

23. About the year 1747, some members of the Society of Quakers, who had become subjects of the revival, formed themselves into a society, of which Jane and James Wardley were the lead. Of this little society Ann Lee and her parents were members. They were all devoutly sincere in the cause of God. James was gifted in public speaking.

24. This infant society practiced no forms, and

adopted no creeds, as rules of faith or worship; but gave themselves up to be led and guided entirely by the operations of the Spirit of God. Their meetings were powerful and animated, and were attended with remarkable signs and operations, and with the spirit of prophecy and Divine revelation.

25. They boldly testified that the second appearing of Christ was at hand; and that the Church would rise in its full and transcendent glory, and effect the final downfall of *antichrist*. They affirmed that the work of the great day of God was then commencing, and would increase, until every promise of God should be fulfilled.

26. Sometimes, after sitting awhile in silent meditation, they were seized with a mighty trembling, under which they would often express the indignation of God against all sin. At other times, they were exercised with singing, shouting, and leaping for joy, at the near prospect of salvation. They were often exercised with great agitation of body and limbs, shaking, running, and walking the floor, with a variety of other operations and signs, swift-

ly passing and repassing each other, like clouds agitated with a mighty wind. These exercises, so strange in the eyes of the beholders, brought upon them the appellation of *Shakers*, which has been their most common name of distinction ever since.

27. They were exposed to much opposition and persecution. Their houses were often beset by mobs, their windows broken, and their persons were shamefully abused. But they bore these things with great patience, and fearlessly continued their assemblies and their testimony. Their meetings, which began in Bolton, near Manchester, were afterward held alternately in Bolton and Manchester; and occasionally at Chester, Mayortown, and some other places in the vicinity of Manchester.

28. They continued to increase in light and power, with occasional additions to their number, till about the year 1770, when, by a special manifestation of Divine light, the present testimony of salvation and eternal life was fully revealed to Ann Lee, and by her to the Society, by whom she, from that time, was acknowledged as *Mother* in Christ, and by them was called *Mother Ann*.

29. Mother Ann said: "I saw in vision the Lord Jesus in his kingdom and glory. He revealed to me the depth of man's loss, what it was, and the way of redemption therefrom. Then I was able to bear an open testimony against the sin that is the root of all evil; and I felt the power of God flow into my soul like a fountain of living water. From that day I have been able to take up a full cross against all the doleful works of the flesh."

30. About the year 1774, Mother Ann received a revelation, directing her to repair to America; also that the second Christian Church would be established in America; that the Colonies would gain their independence; and that liberty of conscience would be secured to all people, whereby they would be able to worship God without hindrance or molestation.

31. This revelation was communicated to the Society, and was confirmed by numerous signs, visions, and extraordinary manifestations, to many of the members; and permission was given for all those of the Society who were able, and who felt

any special impressions on their own minds so to do, to accompany her.

32. Those who became the companions of Mother Ann, in her voyage to America, were: Abraham Stanley (her husband), Wm. Lee (her brother), James Whittaker, John Hocknell, Richard Hocknell (son of John), James Shepherd, Mary Partington, and Nancy Lee (a niece of Mother Ann). Having settled their affairs and made arrangements for the voyage, they embarked at Liverpool, and set sail on the 19th of May, 1774, and debarked on the 6th of August following, at New York.

33. Arrived in America, they settled in the woods, seven miles from Albany, where is now located the village of Watervliet. Here, surrounded by Dutch settlers, they resided three years and a half, waiting for the fulfillment of Mother Ann's prophecy—the *gathering of persons to the Gospel of Christ's second appearing*, of which she was the Messenger.

CHAPTER II.

RISE, PROGRESS, AND PRESENT STATE OF THE SOCIETY.

1. *Community of goods* has never been so successfully accomplished as by the *Shakers*. We propose, therefore, first to take a view of them from that stand-point.

2. *Shakerism as a system* is more varied in its elements, and complex* and expansive in its character, than is any other purely *religious* system within our knowledge, and of course its adherents esteem it as the most perfect and comprehensive; urging as a reason, that *it* takes possession and entire cognizance of the *whole man;* and, instead of attending *solely* to his *spiritual* necessities for

---

* COMPLEX, in the sense of a large "*assemblage*" of ideas, or "*collection*" of elements of truth, "*twisted*" or "wove" together into a unitary system.—WEBSTER.

only *one day in seven*, IT cares for and supplies all his *temporal* as well as *spiritual* wants *seven days in the week.*

3. The physical (not the mere *animal*) and moral, and the intellectual and affectional nature and faculties, together with the *spiritual* as the ruling and governing element, are all to be fully developed and pre-eminently satisfied by the *ultimate* operation of this system, according to the faith and confident expectation of its votaries.

4. In 1779, a very singular and strange revival of religion occurred in the town of New Lebanon, N. Y., and the surrounding country. The people were powerfully and wonderfully exercised in body and soul. Professors of religion who had been the most exemplary and strict in the observance of every means of grace, began to doubt the foundation upon which they had built their hopes of salvation.

5. Some had visions and prophecies that the day of judgment and redemption was at hand, and that the second coming of Christ was nigh—even at the door. In their meetings were heard loud cries for

the kingdom to come, and a powerful testimony against all sin; and the various exercises and gifts of the Spirit gave convincing evidence of its being a genuine work of God.

6. Some, under a deep conviction of their sins, cried for mercy; others felt unspeakably happy in the joyful visions and revelations of the glory of the latter day, and of the commencement of the kindgom of Christ upon earth, which was to put an end to wars and fightings, and all manner of violence, restore peace on earth, make an end of sin, bring in everlasting righteousness, and gather the saints into one harmonious communion.

7. The work was powerful and swift, but of short duration. In a few months their visions and prophecies ceased, the extraordinary power of their testimony seemed to be at an end, and none of those things of which they had testified appeared. In this situation they were filled with deep distress and anxiety of mind, but still retained their confidence in the near approach of Christ's kingdom, and continued their assemblies with earnest prayer and exhortations, encouraging one another to main-

tain their faith and hope, to wait with patience, and to "pray and not faint."

8. This was the state of the people in the spring of 1780, when some of them visited Mother Ann and her little family, and were soon convinced that *they* were in the very work for which themselves had been so earnestly praying, and for which they had been looking and waiting with such ardent expectations.

9. Attracted by the reports of these, others were induced to visit them; and the fame of these strange people, who lived in this obscure corner of the wilderness, extended far and wide. Many from New Lebanon and the country round resorted to them; and when they heard the new and living testimony, and saw the various and extraordinary operations of Divine power among them, they were fully confirmed in the belief that Christ had in very deed appeared again on earth, and many of them (of various denominations) embraced the faith of the Society.

10. Such were some of the preliminary spiritual and religious operations that preceded the organiza-

tion of the Shaker Society at New Lebanon, and are a fair specimen of the manner in which all the succeeding societies originated and have been founded.

11. About the beginning of the present century, another extraordinary revival of religion, known as the "*Kentucky Revival*," commenced in the Western States. This work was also very swift and powerful, and gave such evident proofs of supernatural power, that it excited the attention of all classes of persons, and for a season bore down all opposition. The very astonishing outward operations that attended that work are widely published, and have been the subjects of close and serious investigation.

12. Besides the wonderful operations of spiritual power upon their bodies, the subjects of this work were greatly exercised in dreams, visions, revelations, and the spirit of prophecy. In these gifts of the Spirit they saw and testified that the great day of God was at hand, that Christ was about to set up his kingdom on earth, and that this very work would terminate in the full manifestation of the latter day of glory.

13. This spiritual manifestation extended through several of the Western States, and continued, with increasing light and power, for about four years. During the latter part of the year 1804, many of its subjects were powerfully impressed with a belief that another summer would not pass away without realizing a full display of that great salvation from all sin for which they had been so long and earnestly praying.

14. The Believers in the Eastern States received repeated intelligence of this work through the public papers; and, well remembering the prophecy of Mother Ann, that the next opening of the Gospel would be in the West, they began to look for its speedy fulfillment. This prophecy had often been spoken of while that country was the theater of Indian wars, and it appeared that its fulfillment was near at hand. Accordingly, the next year, the Church at New Lebanon sent three missionaries to them.

15. Without any previous acquaintance in that country, or any correspondence with any of its inhabitants, these messengers, on the first of Janu-

ary, 1805, set out on a pedestrian journey of more than a thousand miles. They arrived in Kentucky about the first of March. They then went to a number of places where the spirit of the revival had prevailed, and conversed with many who had been the subjects thereof; and having, with some freedom, declared the object of their mission, they passed over into the State of Ohio. After visiting and conversing with some of the subjects of the revival in Springfield, they proceeded on to Turtle Creek, near Lebanon, in the county of Warren, whither they arrived on the 22d of March.

16. They were spiritually led to the house of Malcham Worley, a man of respectable character, handsome fortune, liberal education, and who had been a leading character in the revival. Here they felt free to declare their mission, and to open their testimony in full, which Malcham received with great joy, and declared to them that it was the very work that, by the spirit of prophecy, he had been taught to look for.

17. This man had very frequently testified, by the Spirit, that the work of the latter day which

would usher in the kingdom of Christ in that country would commence at that place, which was situated between the two Miama rivers, near Turtle Creek; and there the work did commence, and he and his family were the first to embrace it. From thence it spread, and was cordially received by many of the subjects of the revival in that vicinity, and in a short time it had an extensive circulation through that part of the State, and soon afterward it extended into Kentucky and Indiana, and was joyfully received by many.

18. The testimony mostly prevailed in the States of Ohio and Kentucky, where societies are now established. Many persons from other States, having received the testimony, have become members.

19. In the State of *Ohio* there are *four* societies—one at Union Village, about four miles west from Lebanon, and about 30 miles north-by-east from Cincinnati, Warren County. This is the oldest and largest society in the Western States, and contains about 500 members. The *second* Society is at Watervliet, on Beaver Creek, about

22 miles north from Union Village, and six southeast from Dayton, in Montgomery County, and contains about 100 members.

20. The *third* Society is at Whitewater, 22 miles northwest from Cincinnati, Hamilton County, and contains about 200 members. The *fourth* Society is at North Union, about eight miles northeast from Cleveland, and contains about 200 members.

21. In the State of *Kentucky* there are *two* societies—one at Pleasant Hill, about seven miles easterly from Harrodsburg, and 21 miles southwest from Lexington, Mercer County, which contains between four and five hundred members. The other is at South Union, Jasper Springs, about 15 miles northeast from Russellville, Logan County, and contains between three and four hundred members.

22. There are 18 Shaker Societies, all holding *property in common.* Yet this does not represent the actual number of their community organizations, from the fact, not generally known, that each society is constituted of several distinct fami-

lies, or communities, which are self-supporting, and possess within themselves perfect organizations in both temporal and spiritual matters, regularly officered, comprising elders, deacons, care-takers, etc., of both the *male* and *female* order, agreeably to the unique custom of this singular people, who, although regarded by the world as almost *misogynists* (woman-haters), have been the first to disenthrall woman from the condition of vassalage to which all other religious systems (more or less) consign her, and to secure to her those just and equal rights with man that, by her similarity to him in organization and faculties, both God and nature would seem to demand, inasmuch as the sisterhood is officered and governed throughout by members of their own sex.

23. The Society of New Lebanon possesses *eight* of these families, or communities.

24. The Shaker Societies have not yet extended beyond the boundaries of the " Model Republic;" which is accounted for by the Shakers themselves thus :—They say their religion can not exist and flourish except under such governments as secure

freedom of person, freedom of speech and of the press, liberty of conscience, and perfect separation between church and state.

25. In the public mind an unusual amount of interest attaches to these organizations, from the consideration that among the tens of thousands, in both Europe and America, who (theoretically) as fully indorse the principle of *community of goods*, and approve the abnegation of the private, selfish property principle, as do the " American Shakers" themselves; yet hitherto no attempts to found and perpetuate a community of interest and of goods, and to reconstruct society upon this basis, have proved really successful, except when made under the auspices of, and in accordance with, the peculiar religious requirements of all the combined elements of *Shakerism*.

26. " The full tide of their successful experiments" has already extended itself over seventy years, without a single failure; while the followers of Owen and Fourier have established communities only to awaken hopes that were doomed to be frustrated by their early dissolution; and if any yet

remain, they give marked indications of the winding up of their affairs at no distant period in the future.

27. The oldest and largest Shaker Society is at *New Lebanon*, two miles and a half from Lebanon Springs, and 25 miles southeast of Albany, Columbia County, N. Y. It contains about 600 members.

28. There is also a society at each of the following places, namely:

Watervliet, about seven miles northwest of Albany, N. Y. Members, upward of 300.

Groveland, Livingston County, N. Y., about four miles south of Mount Morris. Members, about 150.

Hancock, three miles from New Lebanon, and five from Pittsfield, Berkshire County, Mass. Members, between two and three hundred.

Tyringham, 16 miles from Hancock, same county and State. Members, about 100.

Enfield, Hartford County, Conn. Members, about 200.

Harvard, Worcester County, Mass. Members, about 200.

Shirley, Middlesex County, Mass. Members, about 100.

Canterbury, Merrimack County, N. H. (near Concord). Members, about 300.

Enfield, Grafton County, N. H. Members, about 300.

Alfred, York County, Maine. Members, about 150.

New Gloucester, Cumberland County, Maine. Members, about 100.

29. These societies were all formed within a period of five years—from 1787 to 1792—and no others were formed until 1805.

30. At the commencement of the year 1780, the whole number of Shakers was only about ten or twelve persons, all of whom came from England. In the spring of that year the American converts began to gather to them, and a gradual accession to their numbers continued until about the year 1785. In 1787, under the superintendence of Joseph Meacham (formerly a Baptist preacher), the people collected together at New Lebanon, and were organized into a community, or church, which

is the pattern and center of union to all the societies, or branches, connected therewith.

31. At that time many of the people were poor in this world's goods, and in debt, and some of them lived in log-houses on the side of the mountain, where now the village of New Lebanon is located.

32. The different communities, or *families*, in each society number from 30 to 150 members, of both sexes, who generally occupy one large unitary dwelling-house, in which the brethren and sisters live together in a spiritual order and social relation, which is the most perfectly represented by a house or family where the parents have numerous sons and daughters.

33. The fact that, in all civilized countries, families are *not* expected to form any other than a brotherly and sisterly union, and which may never, however indirectly, tend toward an *incestuous* conjugal relation, does not prevent their enjoyment of social, friendly intercourse, and a daily interchange of kind offices with each other, there being *other* planes besides the *procreative* for the action of the

affectional nature in males and females, even in the order of natural generation.

34. The *Shakers* testify that they, as a people, find more pleasure and enjoyment—*real good*—arising from the celibate spiritual union of the sexes, and *more of an absence* of the afflictions and annoyances—*real evil*—arising from the generative union of the sexes, than, as they believe, is ever experienced in the order of the world.

35. The apartments of the brethren and sisters are usually at the opposite sides or ends of the house, which is divided by spacious halls. From two to six live in a room. They all eat at the same time, in a large dining-room, at different tables.

36. Each dwelling-house contains a large meeting room, sufficiently spacious to accommodate all the members of the family, in which they assemble several times a week for worship; and twice or thrice a week they have union meetings in their private rooms, where from four to eight or ten brethren and sisters spend an hour, sitting together in social conversation, singing, etc.

37. There are also large buildings, containing

numerous workshops, connected with each family; one for brethren, the other for sisters. In these, various branches of manufacture are carried on, consisting of necessary articles for home consumption and for sale. They have all the mechanical trades necessary to meet the wants of a family. Hitherto, *horticulture* has been the leading business in many of the societies, but they are now turning their attention considerably to *agriculture*.

38. The Society at New Lebanon owns about 6,000 acres of land, a large proportion of which is devoted to fuel, timber, and sheep, it being very mountainous and rocky. The largest part is in the State of Massachusetts. The proportion of land is about ten acres to each individual. Other societies do not vary much from the same ratio.

39. It is now some ten years since the eighteen societies discontinued the use of swine as food. Alcoholic preparations are not drank or used, except under medical advisement. With the Shakers the objects of dress are modesty, health, and comfort; and unless one or other of these objects can be promoted, they never change their fashion.

40. Entire sexual purity, temperance in food and in all other things, plainness and simplicity of dress, neatness, industry, peace, charity to the poor, and a prudent, saving economy in all temporal things, are among the virtues inculcated and practiced by the various fraternities of Shakers, wherever located; all of which greatly tend to promote the physical health and material prosperity of these united societies, and to insure the good-will of their fellow-creatures, and the blessing of Divine Providence upon all their labors.

CHAPTER III.

QUALIFICATIONS FOR MEMBERSHIP, AND RULES AND REGULATIONS.

1. A CONVERT to the faith of *Shakerism*, who wishes to become a Covenant member, is required to pay all his just debts, to discharge all legal obligations upon him, and, if possible, to make restitution for all the wrongs committed against any of his fellow-creatures. A full dedication and consecration of person and property is granted only as a special privilege to such as have been the most faithful to comply with the terms of probation. Nor is any property required as a requisite for admission.

2. No flattery, or any undue influence, is ever used to draw parties into a oneness of temporal interest, as this can be permanently satisfactory

only when it is a voluntary act understandingly performed. Hence the most plain and explicit statements are always laid before the inquirer, so that the whole ground may be fully comprehended by the candidate for admission; for no act of service is considered by this people to be acceptable to God, except it flows from the free, voluntary emotions of the heart. And let the reader bear in mind that all *Shaker* communities are *essentially religious* institutions.

3. No believing husband or wife is allowed to separate from an unbelieving wife or husband, except legally, or by mutual agreement. Nor can any person who has abandoned his or her partner, without just and lawful cause, be received into communion with the Society; and in case of separation between husband and wife, the latter must have a just and righteous share of all property in their possession. Nor are parents allowed to divide their property unequally among their children, whether they be in or out of the Society.

4. The Society is not responsible for debts contracted by persons previous to their becoming

members; and it is expressly contrary to the established principles of the Society for any of its officers, agents, or Covenant members to contract debts, either on behalf of the Society or of themselves individually. All the consecrated property of the Society is held in trust by trustees belonging to each community.

5. As industry, temperance, and frugality are cardinal virtues, all (without exception, if able) are employed in manual labor.

6. The government of the Society is adapted to the several orders of which it is composed; and, not being founded upon force and fraud, as a late Austrian minister of state, Metternich, is reported to have declared all human governments to be, it addresses itself to man's moral and affectional nature. All power and authority under it grow out of the mutual faith, love, and confidence of all its members. It is these that give effective force and power to the principles, laws, rules, and regulations of the Society; and no person who becomes permanently dissatisfied is ever desired to remain in the Society.

7. The societies are divided into different orders, or *classes*, commonly called families.

8. The first, or novitiate class, are those who receive faith and come into a degree of relation with the Society, but choose to live in their own families and manage their own temporal concerns. Any such who choose may live in that manner, and be owned as brethren and sisters in the Gospel, so long as they live up to its requirements.

9. Parents are required to be kind and dutiful to each other; to shun every appearance of evil; to provide for their family; to bring up their children in a godly manner; and to use, improve, and dispose of their property wisely; but may manage their own affairs according to their own discretion. They may continue thus as long as it comports with their faith, circumstances, and spiritual improvement.

10. They are, however, required to bear in mind the necessity and importance of a spiritual increase, without which they will be ever exposed to fall back into the spirit and course of the world; for they can no longer hold their connection with the

Society than they continue to conform to its faith and principles. Such persons are admitted to all the privileges of religious worship and spiritual communion in the novitiate order, and receive instruction and counsel, according to their needs, whenever they feel it necessary to apply for it; and are not debarred from any privilege of which their choice, local situation, and circumstances will admit.

11. Members of this class are not controlled by the Society, with regard to either their property, families, or children, but can act as freely in all these respects as do the members of any other religious society, and yet enjoy all their spiritual privileges, and retain their union with the Society, provided they do not violate the faith and the moral and religious principles of the institution.

12. No children are ever taken under the immediate charge of the Society, except by the request or free consent of those who have the lawful right and control of them, together with the child's own consent. Children thus received are treated with great care and tenderness. The government exer-

cised over them is mild, gentle, and beneficent, which usually excites in them feelings of affection towards one another, and confidence and respect towards their care-takers and teachers, which generally produces a willing obedience in whatever is required of them. The practical exercise of mildness and gentleness of manners is early and sedulously cultivated.

13. Children are early led into the knowledge of the sacred Scriptures, instructed in their history, and practically taught the divine precepts contained in them, particularly those of Jesus Christ and his Apostles. They are also brought up to some manual occupation suited to their capacities, by which to be enabled to obtain a livelihood, whether they remain with the Society or not.

14. Of Shaker *schools*, we will simply give an extract from the " Report of the Select Committee of the Legislative Assembly of the State of New York, April 2d, 1849 :"—

" On examining the schools at Watervliet (a fair specimen of those in the other societies), a model worthy the imitation of the best society was presented. A full and excellent library of the most approved books was found, and a thorough education for the business man is there imparted, by teachers who are competent for the task. The scholars, both male and female, seemed highly pleased with their situation, and were in the apparent enjoyment of all the pleasures of youthful life."

15. The second, or *Junior Class*, is composed of persons who, not having the charge of families, and being under no embarrassments to hinder them from uniting in community order, choose to enjoy the benefits of that situation. These enter into a contract to devote their services freely to support the interest of the family of which they may be members, so long as they shall continue in that order, at the same time stipulating to claim no pecuniary compensation for their services. Every member of such family is benefited by the united interest and labors of the whole family, so long as they continue to support the order thereof, and is amply provided for in health, sickness, and old age.

16. Members of this class have the privilege, at their option, of freely giving the improvement of any part, or all, of their property, to be used for the mutual benefit of the family to which they belong. The property itself may be resumed at any time, according to the contract, but no interest can be claimed for the use thereof; nor can any member of the family be employed therein for *wages* of any kind.

17. Members of this class may retain the lawful ownership of all their own property as long as they think proper; and at any time, after having gained sufficient experience to be able to act deliberately and understandingly, they may, if they choose, dedicate and devote a part or the whole, and consecrate it forever to the support of the institution. This, however, is a matter of *free choice*.

18. The third, or *Senior Class*, is composed of such persons as have had sufficient time and opportunity practically to prove the faith and manner of life of the Society, and who are prepared to enter freely, fully, and voluntarily into a united and conse-

crated interest. These covenant and agree to devote themselves and services, with all they possess, to the service of God, and the support of the Gospel, forever, solemnly promising never to bring debt or damage, claim or demand, against the Society, or against any member thereof, for any property or service they may thus have devoted to the uses and purposes of the institution. This class constitutes what is denominated *Church Order*.

19. To enter fully into this order is considered a matter of the utmost importance to the parties concerned, and therefore requires the most mature and deliberate consideration; for, after having made such a dedication, according to the laws of justice and equity, there can be no ground for retraction; nor can any one, by those laws, recover anything thus dedicated. Of this all are fully apprised before they enter into the order. Yet should any afterwards withdraw from the Society, the trustees have discretionary power to give them what may be thought reasonable. No person who withdraws peaceably is ever sent away empty.

20. During a period of seventy years, since the

permanent establishment of the Society at New Lebanon and Watervliet, there has never been a legal claim entered by any person for the recovery of property brought into the Society.

21. The members of this order are all entitled to equal benefits and privileges, and no difference is ever made on account of the property any individual may have contributed.

22. The following extract from a charge to a jury, delivered by the Hon. John Breathitt, of Kentucky, shows the light in which the "Covenant" of the Senior Order has been viewed in a court of justice:

> "And is it matter of objection against any man that his motives are so pure and disinterested that he desires to be released from earthly thraldom, that he may fix all his thoughts and affections on his God? After they have signed the Covenant, they are relieved from earthly care.
>
> "I repeat it: *That* individual who is prepared to sign the Church Covenant stands in an enviable situation. His situation, indeed, is

an enviable one, who, devoted to his God, is prepared to say of his property, Here it is, little or much, take it, and leave me unmolested to commune with my God. Indeed, I dedicate myself to—what?—not to a fanatical tenet!—O no! to a subject far beyond—to the worship of Almighty God, the great Creator and Governor of the universe. Under the influence of his love I give my *all:* only let me worship according to my faith and in a manner I believe to be acceptable to my God.

"I say again: The world can not produce a parallel to the situation which such a man exhibits—resigned to the will of Heaven, free from all the feelings of earthly desire, and quietly pursuing the even tenor of his way."

23. We believe the history of the world does not furnish a single instance of any other religious institution having stood 70 years without a visible declension of its principles and order, and in the general purity and integrity of its members.

24. An institution with a united interest in all things has been a *desideratum* of the world for

many ages; and although attempts to establish such have been made in various ages and countries, apparently under favorable circumstances and well-adapted plans, yet they have as often failed; while the central society of this community has stood upon the ground of a united and consecrated interest, and maintained the institution of equal rights and privileges in all things, both spiritual and temporal, for more than 70 years, without the least appearance of failure in either the parent Society, or any of its branches.

25. *Well-defined fixed principles*, that are perfectly understood and cordially received by all the members, constitute the *foundation* of the *Shaker government*.

26. Growth is secured and progress effected by a continual influx of light and love from the Fountain—*God*—by means of Divine revelation through spirits. The rulers are but the executive of the principles above referred to, and of the laws deduced therefrom. Their means, and the object, of government consist in bringing the principles so approved to bear upon the consciences and

affections of the ruled. To this end the male and female elements are equally balanced in the leaders. The *former* has reference to, and operates more specifically upon, the *rational* faculty in human nature; the *latter*, to the *affectional*.

27. The Ministry, who are the central executive of the whole order, consists of two brethren and two sisters, and every regularly organized community or family in a society has two *elder* brethren and two *elder* sisters, who have the charge of the *spiritual* affairs; also, two deacons and two deaconesses, who have the care of the *temporalities*. All other positions of care and trust are filled after the same *dual* order. Yet each sex continues in its own appropriate sphere of action in all respects, there being a proper subordination, deference, and respect of the female to the male, *in his order*, and of the male to the female, *in her order*; so that in any of these communities the zealous advocates of "Woman's Rights" may here find a practical realization of their *ideal*.

28. To the mind of the simple, unsophisticated

Shaker it seems marvelously inconsistent for any human government to be administered for the sole benefit of its own officers and their particular friends and favorites; or that more than one half the citizens should be disfranchised because they happen to be *females*, and compelled by the sword to obey laws they never sanctioned, and ofttimes in which they have no faith, and to submit to taxation where there has been no previous representation; while still millions of other fellow-citizens are treated as *property*, because they chance to possess a darker-colored skin than their cruel brethren. And again, that the members (*brethren and sisters*) of the same religious body or church should be divided into *rich* and *poor* in the things of this temporary world, but who are vainly expecting that, in the world to come, they shall be *willing* to have eternal things *in common!*

29. And when this same unjust and unequal administration is confirmed and carried out in the most popular religious organizations of Christendom, the Shakers think the climax of absurdity, tyranny, and oppression well-nigh attained.

CHAPTER IV.

CHARACTERISTICS AND DOCTRINES OF JESUS CHRIST.

1. CHRIST was "the Author and Finisher of the faith" of Christianity; and in Jesus Christ was the first Christian Church, which was perfect and prolific *spiritually* just so far as Adam was perfect and prolific naturally, before Eve was brought forth.

2. Christ (dual) is a supermundane being, and was the Agent of the *new revelation* to Jesus, the truths of which were, *first*, the immortality of the soul, which Moses never taught; and, *second*, the resurrection of the soul—these being two distinct things; the former, the continuous existence of the soul after mere physical death; the latter, the quickening of the germ of a new and spiritual life in the soul, consequent upon, and succeeding to, the death of the first Adamic or generative life, which

can only be effected by the faith and the cross of the second Adam—*Christ*.

3. As all the future powers and faculties of the natural man are germinal in the infant, so the life and faculties of the future spiritual man are germinal in the soul of the natural or "old" man; and these are never quickened, except by the same power that destroys the *life* of the "old man"—the desire of generation. "I wound, and I heal; I kill, and I make alive." These are the two lives that Jesus alluded to when he said, "Whosoever will save his *life* shall lose *it;* and whosoever will lose his *life* for my sake shall find it, and keep it unto life eternal."

4. The prophet Isaiah, speaking of Jesus, says: "His *life* was cut off from the *earth;* and who shall declare *his generation?*" Meaning that his earthly life, which supports the work of generation, was "cut off," as must be also the *earthly life* of every true Christian. And Jesus himself said: "Therefore doth my Father love me, because *I lay down my life.* No man taketh it from me; but *I lay it down of myself.*"

5. The beginning of Christianity was the end of generation—of the world—in Jesus. "Ye are they [said the Apostle] upon whom the ends of the world *have come*" already. Thus the same Spirit that creates souls "anew in Christ Jesus," causes them to "forsake and to hate father and mother, wife and children, brothers and sisters, houses and land, and their own [generative] life also." This hitherto paradoxical and hard saying of Jesus, the Shakers simplify upon the above premises, affirming that all these characters can be hated without the least enmity against any human soul.

6. It is the generative life in man and woman that induces them to assume the character of *husband and wife;* the same life impels them to become father and mother; and hence result the *children*, who are *brothers and sisters*, all of whom require, desire, and (if they can) acquire *houses and land*, to support the earth-relation thus formed. All these can be forsaken and hated without hating the persons of the original man and woman, or of the children.

7. It is the earthly, fleshly *relation* that must be hated by all who would become followers of Jesus—*Christians*—" children of the resurrection," of whom Jesus said, "They neither marry nor are given in marriage, but are *as* the angels of God in heaven."

8. All who "marry and are given in marriage," or who support that order, the Shakers term "the children of this world;" thus, on this ground, throwing heathens, Turks, Catholics, Protestants, infidels, etc., all into one general class, or company. They quote Jesus: "Think not that I am come to bring peace on *earth* [to the earthly procreative relation]; for I am come to set a man at variance against his father, and the daughter against her mother, and the daughter-in-law against her mother-in-law, and to make a man's foes those of his own household."

9. Yet the Shakers do not condemn marriage as an institution of "the world," to whom only it belongs; but they say that the procreative powers should be used by them exclusively for offspring, and that all beyond that, however perfectly it may

be covered by the mantle of *human law*, they call "the unfruitful works of darkness."

10. "He that looks upon a woman to lust after her, has [in the sight of God] committed adultery with her" none the less because she is his legal wife. God looks at the *impelling motive*, not the *human legality*, of an action. "Blessed are [*not* the legal, but] the *pure* in heart, for they shall see God."

11. Those who will "crucify the old man, with all his *affections* and *lusts*, shall see a greater manifestation of God than it is possible for a generative man to behold; to prove which, the Shakers adduce *scientific* no less than *scriptural* reasons. "The natural man *discerneth not* the things of the Spirit; neither can he know them," any more than fishes can see and know the things pertaining to *land* animals, or than the chrysalis can be cognizant of the fields and flowers of the future butterfly.

12. *Second.* Another practical principle, in which Christ instructed Jesus, was *Brotherhood*—to love his neighbor as himself, and not to appro-

priate to his own selfish use, to the exclusion of those on the same plane, either of the life-elements —earth, air, fire, or water. Foxes had holes in the ground, and birds nests in the trees, but Jesus had no place or home to call his own.

13. And except a man forsook all that he had, he could not be a disciple of Jesus. Hence the rich young man went sorrowful away, rather than sell and distribute his great possessions, and thus become a poor man, in order to join Jesus and his company. This also explains why a cable could go through the eye of a needle easier than a *rich* man could enter into the kingdom of heaven, which was formed within, or among his disciples.

14. Five dollars of private, *selfish* property would exclude a man from the communion of a company who, as did Jesus and his Apostles, possessed their property *in common*, as effectually as would five millions; for the law of the Gospel is, " Except a man forsake all that he hath, he can not enter into the kingdom of heaven." In addition to that, he must also follow the example of

Jesus, in "taking up the cross," and living a virgin life.

15. The *third* principle exemplified in the life of Jesus, and which came from the same source as the preceding ones, is, "Resist not evil"—*non-resistance.* "If any man smite thee on thy right cheek, turn to him the other also. Love your enemies. Do good to them that hate you. Bless them that curse you." "He that taketh the sword shall perish by the sword." "The Son of man is not come to destroy men's lives, but to save them." So that, according to Shaker doctrines, there can be no such thing as a *Christian* warrior. With them the time has come to beat the sword into a plowshare, and the spear into a pruning-hook, and they will not practise or learn war any more.

16. *Fourth.* Jesus took no part in earthly governments. When he was offered all the kingdoms of the world for his possession, he utterly refused them, and thus crucified his ambition. He also taught his disciples that, although "the princes of the Gentiles exercise dominion over

them, and they that are great exercise authority upon them, it shall not be so among you; for whosoever will be great and chief among you, let him be your minister—servant—least of all."

17. *Fifth.* Christ saved Jesus from sin; and "*his* name was called Jesus, because he should save *his* people from *their* sins." Hence the Shakers claim a *present salvation from sin* as essential to the Christian character. They say that the Law of Moses (in respect to salvation) was "weak through the flesh" (generation), which it allowed at the same time that it condemned all who practised it.

18. For it enjoined that "the man who shall lay with a woman . . . . was unclean;" that they were "both unclean"—*sinful:* and "the bed whereon they lay was unclean," or defiled; and they were separated from the camp of Israel therefor. Nor could they be again admitted until they had been re-baptized (washed all over) with water.

19. Jesus escaped this only by living "separate from sin and sinners;" that is, by living a virgin

life. If *he* had married, and lived in generation, he must have been subject to the Law as above stated, and paid the penalty; for he "came not to destroy the Law, but to fulfill" the righteousness thereof.

20. John the Baptist told the soldiers to "do violence to no man." And the Jewish Apostle said, "Marriage is honorable in all, if the bed be undefiled." The sin was not in being a soldier, but in *doing violence;* nor was the sin in the fact of marriage, but in the *act* of generation; for persons may have been married before being called to be Christians, as was the case with Peter and others.

21. The penal law was added because of transgression; the *typical* law, of baptism, circumcision, etc., to foreshadow things to come. The latter was abolished by the substance—*virgin life;* and the former, by "ceasing to do evil, and learning to do well." There could be no sin-offering where there was no sin; no type, when the antetype had come; and no tithes, where there was no *individual* property, but "all things common."

CHAPTER V.

CHARACTER OF THE PRIMITIVE CHRISTIAN CHURCH.

1. JESUS CHRIST foretold two things of great importance. *One* was, that the Christian Church, which he originated, would not continue, but would be utterly destroyed. He said that himself and his disciples were " the light of the world;" and he counselled souls to walk in the light while they had it, because " the night cometh wherein no man can work." That is, there would come a time when " iniquity would abound, and the love of many would wax cold," and when there would be no true Church on the earth. The same was confirmed by his Apostles, who said there would be a " falling away," and that " that man of sin would be *revealed*," in place of a revelation of Christ.

2. The *other* was, that another appearing on

earth of the same Christ (or second Adam and Eve) as had been manifested to him (Jesus) would take place, to establish a second and more perfect Christian Church, precisely according to the Pattern of the Christian Church *in himself;* for then Christ would come, not in *one* individual only, but "in the clouds of [the fourth] heaven, with power and great glory;" that is, in *numbers* of persons, or "clouds of witnesses," in and among whom Christ would make his "second appearing without sin unto salvation." "Behold the Lord cometh in ten thousand of his saints."

3. For the Shaker idea is, that in Jesus alone were all the characteristics of a perfect Christian; that the Apostles stood upon a *lower* plane, and were children of God by "*adoption*" only, *not really*. This point is conclusively proved from the conjoint testimony of themselves and Jesus.

4. Jesus said he had "many things to say unto them that they were not able to bear," and exclaimed of them, "O ye of little faith!" These expressions, with the mistaken conceptions the

Apostles had formed of the nature of his kingdom and of the resurrection, demonstrate that they only "knew in part, prophesied in part, and saw as through a glass darkly" and imperfectly.

5. The Apostles were "only a *kind* of first-fruits;" not the kingdom itself. But they had the spirit of promise and of hope, that in the second appearing, when Christ should be manifested in the order of *Mother*, through a *female*, as he had been in the order of *Father*, through *Jesus*, they should sit down with Jesus on his throne—rise to the same plane.

6. This was the condition and expectation of the Apostolic Church, whose members were all Hebrews. For, as Maria Childs remarks, "Christianity was somewhat exclusive and national in its character, being preached only by Jesus, and addressed only to Hebrews."

7. The Church professed to live a virgin life; and those in it who "waxed wanton against Christ," and *married*, had "damnation, because they had cast off their first faith" of *celibacy*. "They had all things common." The 8,000 who

were converted in two days "sold all their possessions" of houses and land, and formed a perfect community. They did not call the least thing their "*own*." They took no part in the heathen governments, either in being officers or electing officers. They would not swear, or take oaths. They would not fight, or engage in war; and they suffered much persecution because they would not enlist in the armies of the Roman empire.

8. They bore a testimony against sin, saying, "He who sinneth hath not seen Christ, neither known him." They had the gift of healing the sick. "Is any sick among you? let him send for the elders of the Church," etc.; and often their shadow or their clothes imparted a healing power to the invalid. They "looked for the second appearing of Christ, and hasted unto the coming of the day of the Lord."

9. This was the *Jewish* Christian Church, the temple of God, and was founded by the Apostles one degree below the Church in Jesus. And when Peter preached Christianity to the Gentiles, he founded the *Gentile* Christian Church on a plane

still lower than that of the *Jewish* Christian Church.

10. The *Gentile* Christian Church did not introduce war or slavery, but it did introduce *marriage* and *private property;* yet both these institutions were under restrictions drawn from the Mosaic laws, to which the Gentiles had never been accustomed. They were restricted to *one* wife, and subjected to self-denial in many respects; that was all they were able to bear. But they were not saved from sin; and they looked for the second coming of Christ, when, as the Apostle told them, those who had wives would be just the same as if they were not married; and those who owned property, as though they possessed nothing; as then they would rise into the order of the Church above them.

11. The Shaker writers say that unless this distinction between the *Jewish* Christian Church and the *Gentile* Christian Church be observed, the various writings of the New Testament can not be understood, as all the Epistles to the Gentile Christian Churches contain very different doc-

trines to those addressed to the Hebrews, and as contained in the four Gospels. The Gentile Christians were fed with "milk, and not with meat, because they were not able to bear it." They were written to "as unto carnal, and not as unto spiritual."

12. The five most prominent practical principles of the Pentecost Church were, first, *common property;* second, *a life of celibacy;* third, *non-resistance;* fourth, a *separate* and *distinct government;* and, fifth, *power over physical disease.*

CHAPTER VI.

FALL OF THE PRIMITIVE CHRISTIAN CHURCH.

1. WHEN Constantine was converted, he founded and became the *heathen** head of the *Roman Catholic* Church, which was formed upon a very much lower plane than was even the *Gentile* Christian Church.

2. It was distinguished from that, *first,* by the union of church and state, the Church gradually

---

* Constantine, who was a *heathen*, was *never* converted to even Roman Catholic Christianity. Mosheim says of him: "It is certain that he was *not received* by baptism into the number of the faithful *until a few days before his death*," and then only in order that he "might ascend pure and spotless to the mansions of light and immortality;" notwithstanding his having cruelly murdered his father-in-law, his wife, his son, his brother-in-law, his nephew, and others, besides his numerous other abominations. (See Mosheim's Ecclesiastical History, by Dr. Maclaine, American edition, 1797, vol. i., cent. iv., part i., chap. i., pp. 313, 314.)

assuming the supreme power and control of all civil as well as ecclesiastical matters; *second*, by the introduction of war as a permanent element of theology, using the sword not only against *external* enemies of the church and state, but as a means of conversion to Roman Catholic Christianity, and also turning the same sword against the *internal* enemies of this mongrel church and its theology, by the establishment of the *inquisition*, based upon the absurd idea that faith, or want of faith, is the result of the *will*, and *not of evidence*, or the absence thereof; by *monopoly* of the elements of existence, particularly of the earth and its produce; by *slavery*, which was also incorporated into the Church as a part of its theological creeds; and by *oaths*.

3. The Roman Catholic Church is the "beast" that John saw, which combined the wild, destructive characteristics of the bear, the leopard, and the lion.

4. And John was commanded to "rise and measure the temple of God [the *Jewish* Christian Church] and them that worship therein. But the

court, which is without, measure it not; for it is given unto the Gentiles [the *Gentile* Christian Church]; and they shall tread down the holy city forty-and-two months"—1,260 years.

5. That was the falling away and degenerating of the *Gentile* Christian Church into the *Roman Catholic* Church; and the union of church and state, with the adoption of war, possessed it of physical power, by which means it trod down liberty of conscience, requiring the *Jewish* Christian Church to come to its standard of orthodoxy, or endure physical torture, and the breaking up of their communities, by the operation of its oppressive organic laws.

6. John also "saw a beast, great and terrible [as above described], rise out of the sea"—the spiritual elements of the Primitive Church. "This beast [the Roman Catholic Church] made war with the saints, and overcame them; and all the world wondered [and wandered] after the beast." And he ruled over all nations, kindreds, tongues, and people, and there was no power on earth able to wage war with this beast; therefore it

is plain that *that church* is the beast of the Apocalypse.

7. And John "saw another beast rise out of the *earth* [Rationalism and Materialism], having two horns like a lamb, but spoke with the mouth of a dragon." This was the "image of the first beast; and it exercised all the power of the first beast," war, persecution, etc. This is *Protestantism*, in which Lutheranism and Calvinism are the two principal powers (or horns), for they divide the kingdom of the "image of the beast" between them.

8. In no one important practical principle of life did the Protestant Church differ from the Roman Catholic Church. Both of them hold to marriage, private property, union of church and state, ambition, oaths, persecution, war, slavery, monopoly of the life-elements in its most aggravated form; salvation, an unmeaning something to be possessed in some distant, unknown world, but gained and secured in this by means of water, bread, wine, blood, and belief in the cruel murder of the best man the earth ever produced, or faith in the wooden cross, the instrument of his cruci-

fixion. And both alike inherit all the diseases of the Egyptians, and (as churches) are utterly destitute of the gift of healing, as well as of all the other gifts that were possessed by the Primitive Church.

9. Thus the "beast which ruled over all nations, kindreds, people, and tongues," and "the great Whore of Babylon, the Mother of Harlots and of abominations of the earth, who sitteth upon many waters" (and "the waters where the whore sitteth are peoples, and multitudes, and nations, and tongues"), are the one and the same *Roman Catholic Church*. She is the "woman," the "great city that ruleth over the kings of the earth" for forty-and-two months; and her endless brood of harlot daughters, "hateful, and hating one another," are the divided, warring *Protestant sects*.

10. And the mother and her daughters, for want of a common enemy, bite, rend, and devour each other; and, in their jarring creeds, they not only "teach for doctrines the commandments of men," but they teach even the "doctrines of

devils," as before enumerated; and, by external laws, "forbidding to marry"—the counterfeit of a virgin life; and "commanding to abstain from meats"—the counterfeit of true temperance in all things, the legitimate fruit of the testimony of Jesus; "preaching for hire, and divining for money"—a fictitious Gospel that is *not* "without money and without price."

11. Therefore Christendom (Babylon) "has become the habitation of devils [demons, or disorderly disembodied spirits, who are ministers of falsities and confusion], the hold of every foul spirit, and the cage of every hateful and unclean bird." For there is no form of human wickedness which can not be found within the pale of the theological organizations of Christendom.

12. That the Protestant Reformation effected a revolution for the better, the Shakers do not question; nor that even Roman Catholicism itself is an advance upon mere heathenism; for the laws of progress will assert their supremacy in all human affairs, and God can make (or overrule) even the *wrath of man* to praise Him.

13. Adjudged from the stand-point of the people and age upon whom, and in which, they operated, both Constantine, Luther, and Calvin were real reformers; but adjudged from the stand-point of Jesus and his seven principles (true Christianity), they were what Luther, in his last will and testament, subscribed himself as being, "a damnable man," and as both Catholics and Protestants say of themselves, "miserable sinners."

CHAPTER VII.

RISE OF THE "TWO WITNESSES."

1. NEXT in order come the "two witnesses," who were to "prophesy [and mourn and repent] in sackcloth and ashes," during the forty-two months' reign of the beast and his image.

2. Although the "holy city," or *Jewish* Christian Church, was trodden down by the Roman Catholic, or *fallen Gentile* Christian Church (antichrist), yet God, by revelation, raised up in every age of the apostasy *male* and *female* witnesses, who, reviving the principles or testimony of the *Jewish* Christian Church, as already set forth, testified, or witnessed, against the beast and his image, by word and by their lives of innocence. They held no union with church or state; they took no oaths, bore no arms, held no slaves, lived a virgin life, and "had all things common."

3. These were the "holy people," whose power was continually scattered by the persecuting arm of antichrist. They were known to their enemies by the term "heretics," and by historians as Marcionites, Therapeutics, Manicheans, Nestorians, Waldenses, Moravians, etc., and, lastly, as Quakers, who, with the exception of a virgin life, embodied more of the principles of the Primitive Church than any other of the "witnesses."

4. It has been estimated that fifty millions of these "witnesses," or "heretics," have been tortured to death by the *Inquisition*, and other instrumentalities of the terrible beast, or Roman Catholic Church; and, by the image of the beast, a proportionate number.

5. The full history of the rise and fall of these "witnesses," should such ever be impartially written, would prove a highly interesting record. Each of them "began in the Spirit." They originated in a revelation to some man or woman, as Marcion, Manes, Priscillian, Fox, Joanna Southcott, Jemima Wilkinson, and others. When they had " finished their testimony, the beast made war

against them, and killed them; but they would not suffer the *dead bodies* to be put into graves," but left them lying in the streets of his city of Babylon; and thus the "kingdom of the beast has become full of names" (they are numbered by hundreds) of sects who have lost their spiritual life, finished their testimony against sin, and have given their power and influence unto the kingdom of the beast, by uniting with, and building up, the very things they formerly took up their cross against.

6. Persecution continued while their testimony lasted, and they grew in grace and truth. It was when the church and state began to favor and speak well of them that concessions became mutual —then it was that they were "killed" *spiritually*, and not by persecution.

7. The *monks* and *nuns* are some of the "dead bodies" of the Roman Catholic Church; and the Dunkers, Waldenses, Baptists, Methodists, and Quakers (who may be taken as a type of all the witnesses) are some of the "dead bodies" of the Protestant Church.

8. It was this unbroken chain of "witnesses"

that connected the first and second Christian Churches. At the end of the 1,260 years, "the Spirit of life from God" entered into some individual "witnesses" of that "dead body" called *Quakers*, and "they stood upon their feet," or spiritual understandings, "and they heard a voice from [the resurrection plane of the fourth] heaven, saying, Come up hither;" and they obeyed it; "and they ascended up to heaven in a cloud," or body; and they have dwelt in heaven more than 70 years; for the kingdom of heaven is formed "within," or among, "them." They have the testimony of Jesus, and they live in a more perfect Christian order, and possess a greater gift of salvation from sin, than did the *Jewish* Christian Church at Jerusalem.

9. As John preached repentance unto *Moses*, to prepare souls for Christ's first appearing, so did Fox, and Jane and James Wardley preach repentance unto Christ's *first* appearing, to prepare souls for the *second* coming of Christ, and the setting up of his final kingdom upon earth.

10. Thus, out of the last of the "witnesses,"

the Quakers, the "forty-and-two months" having expired, arose *Ann Lee* and her little company, to whom Christ appeared the *second* time, " without sin unto salvation," and made a new revelation to her of the seven principles, and of all the truths that had been revealed, in his *first* appearing, to *Jesus ;* the practice of which constituted *him* the *first Christian Church ;* and the same principles being reduced to practice by *Ann Lee*, constituted *her* the *second Christian Church.*

11. The "marriage of the Lamb had come, for his wife had *made herself* ready [thus showing that she was not *born* ready]; and to her was given to be arrayed in fine linen, clean and white: the fine linen was the *righteousness of saints*," nothing more.

12. *Ann*, by strictly obeying the light revealed within her, became "righteous even as Jesus was righteous." She acknowledged Jesus Christ as her Head and Lord, and formed the same character as a *spiritual woman* that he formed as a *spiritual man.*

13. *Ann followed Jesus*, not as an imitator,

but through being baptized with, and led by, the same Christ Spirit that he was baptized with and led and guided by. She became a Mother in Israel, and was thenceforth known to her followers (or children) by the endearing name of *Mother*. Still it was the principles (before explained) that were the *foundation* of the second Christian Church, and not man or woman, whether Jesus or Ann. Their importance is derived from the fact of *their* being the *first* man and the *first woman* perfectly identified with the principles and Spirit of Christ.

14. A part of the curse pronounced upon *woman* was, that *man* should *rule over her*, which has been fully accomplished; for, from the fall to the present time, all human governments have claimed it to be the sole right of the *man* to "rule," whether in religious or political organizations, and Christian churches and governments (so called) have been no real exception to this *rule*.

15. As Christ's *first* appearing was only to and in the *male* part of humanity, the *Jewish* as well

as the *Gentile* Christian Churches were governed almost entirely by *men*. The Roman Catholic and Protestant world know only *male* rulers; *woman* is ignored. The Quakers, the last of the "witnesses," began to include the *female* element in their system; but not until Christ had made his *second* appearance in and to the *female*, was woman ever allowed a full and equal share in any civil or religious government, or established in the possession of her just and equal rights.*

16. Naturalists state that the larvæ of the common working bee, by simply feeding it upon superior food, can be progressed to a *queen bee*. This, if true, proves that every such bee possesses the undeveloped germ of a queen bee, and is a beautiful figure of the spiritual life that is *hid* with every natural man and woman, "hid with Christ in God," waiting the second advent of Christ, to

---

* The fact that females sometimes reign over nations as queens, is only an *apparent* exception to the above rule and practice, it being so only in case of default of *male* issue; for they do not reign as *women*, and over *females only*, but *as men*, instead of men, and over men, which, *as women*, is *not their right*.

feed and quicken it into being, on a plane above that of the earthly animal order of generative reproduction.

17. This is the true *resurrection* state in which Jesus stood when he said, "I am the resurrection." To this state Paul desired to arrive when he said, "I follow after, if that by any means I may attain to the resurrection from the dead." This could not mean the re-animation of the physical body, as that (if true) would be as independent of the will as was its physical birth or death. A physical resurrection, the Shakers hold to be utterly repugnant to both science, reason, and Scripture.

CHAPTER VIII.

CHARACTER OF THE CHURCH OF CHRIST'S SECOND APPEARING.

1. IN the fourteenth chapter of the book of the Revelation, the second appearing of Christ is described as already past. The hundred and forty-four thousand mentioned are not a particular number; it is a Hebraism, denoting a perfect character by numbers, as 12×12, a perfect *square:* they are *virgins;* they are redeemed from the earth, from among men; they "follow the Lamb [Jesus] whithersoever he goeth;" they are without fault or sin, and they have the everlasting Gospel to preach to them that dwell upon the earth.

2. An angel proclaims the fall of Babylon, as the effect of the preaching of the Gospel. Another angel denounces a woe upon those who have the "*mark of the beast*"—the seal of authority placed

upon the organ of *causality* preventing the action of the reasoning faculties.

3. There is the "*white cloud*"—a sinless, innocent company—upon which "*one* sat *like unto the Son of man;*" for as Eve was like unto Adam—"bone of his bone, and flesh of his flesh"—so was Mother Ann like unto Jesus—of the human race, of the same origin, life, character, and principles.

4. The "*sharp sickle,*" with which another angel "reaped the ripe harvest of the earth," is the *testimony of Jesus*—the everlasting Gospel—which cuts souls off from the field of *generation*, and thus (in them) brings the world to an end.

5. The angel alluded to in the eighteenth chapter, who "came down from heaven, having great power, and the earth was lightened with his glory," and who proclaimed the fall of Babylon, is *Spiritualism*. The *physical* manifestations exhibit the power of the invisible over the visible world, the light of which is to enlighten the earth—*materialists*—by leading them to a knowledge of the immortality of the soul, of the existence of a spirit-

world, of the fact of the intercommunication between the two worlds, and of the rights of man.

6. Spiritualism can minister physical power and spiritual light, but *not* a knowledge of the way of salvation from sin. It can confound earthly and religious materialists, and reveal the false doctrines of *antichrist*, of which itself is an integral part, and thus accelerate her fall; but it is not able to re-arrange society.

7. The Spirit is indeed being "poured out upon all flesh," without distinction of age, sex, party, or even *moral condition*. But it comes to pass that only such as "call upon the name of the Lord shall be saved." For in Jerusalem, and in Mount Zion alone, is deliverance from the *power of sin*.

8. And the *one* sitting upon the "white cloud," from whose face the heavens and the earth—the old religious and civil systems of Babylon—"fled away," and who is "like Jesus," *she* possesses that power, and utters a voice to those in falling Babylon: "Come out of her, my people, that ye be not partakers of her sins, and that ye receive not of her plagues."

9. And those who hear the voice of "the Spirit" (Christ Jesus) and of "the Bride" (Mother Ann) form the "new heaven and the new earth, wherein dwells righteousness." And they build the tabernacle of God, which is with men; "and God Himself shall dwell with them, and shall be their God, and they shall be his people." All this the Shakers believe, and hold is fulfilled, or being fulfilled, *in their order—its* faith, principles, and communities.

10. "For now has come salvation and strength, the kingdom of our God, and the power of his Christ." For the tyrant, *lust*, "the accuser of the brethren" in all the three preceding Dispensations, is now cast out; "and the ransomed of the Lord have come to Zion, with singing, and with everlasting joy upon their heads."

CHAPTER IX.

MODE OF WORSHIP.

1. It is pretty generally known that the Shakers serve God by singing and dancing; but *why* they practise this mode of worship is not so generally understood.

2. It should be recollected that "God is a Spirit," and can be worshiped only "in spirit and in truth." Without the presence of the Spirit there can be no true worship. Conviction of sin, godly sorrow, and repentance, are the first effects of the Spirit of God upon the conscience of a sinner. And when sin is fully removed, by confessing and forsaking it, the *cause* of heaviness, gloom, and sorrow is gone; and joy and rejoicing, and thanksgiving and praise, are then the spontaneous effects of a true spirit of devotion. And whatever

manner the Spirit may dictate, or whatever the *form* into which the Spirit may lead, it is acceptable to Him from whom the Spirit proceeds.

3. All the *sabbaths* among the Jews, as hereafter set forth, were joyous festivals—times for men to do good to each other, by feeding the hungry, clothing the naked, etc.; for all to make each other happy, and thus rejoice before the Lord, " with music and dancing."

4. Dancing was a national custom among the Hebrews upon all extraordinary occasions of some great good, as a victory, etc. They expressed their satisfaction and happiness by *dancing*, as the Americans do by the abnegation of temperance, and the explosion of gunpowder.

5. When Israel had escaped the Egyptians, " all the women went after Miriam with timbrels, and with dances." The virgins of Israel held a yearly feast at Shiloh, with dances. When David killed Goliath there was dancing. " And David danced with all his might before the ark of the Lord."

6. Dancing is often mentioned by the seers,

prophets, and prophetesses. "Thou hast turned my mourning into dancing." "Praise his name in the dance." "Praise him with the timbrel and dance." When the prophets spoke of the Millennial period and Church, it was with expressions such as, "Then shall the *virgin* rejoice in the dance, both old men and young together." "O virgin of Israel, thou shalt go forth in the dances of them that make merry." And Jesus, in speaking of the return of the prodigal son, included music and dancing as a part of the proceedings and rejoicing.

7. But so plain and simple a subject does not require much extension or amplification. Suffice it to say, that the Shakers believe the great "*sabbatical year*" of the world has come, wherein the long captive sinner is released; "the poor have the Gospel preached to them, without money and without price;" perpetual and universal brotherhood is established and proclaimed, each one (as Jesus said) going back to his inheritance in the earth: "Blessed are the meek, for they shall inherit the earth," and all things else, *in com-*

mon, as an everlasting Jubilee of jubilees, where the rich and the poor, the high and the low, the bond and the free, male and female, all become *one* in Christ Jesus; and *love* is the bond of their union.

CHAPTER X.

DOCTRINES OF THE CHURCH OF CHRIST'S SECOND APPEARING.

PART I.

MOSAIC SABBATHS, AND HIGHER AND LOWER LAW.

1. As a common schoolmaster teaches the rudiments which form the basis of the knowledge to be acquired in the higher seminaries of learning, so was Moses to Christ.

2. Moses, as did all the other Prophets, announced the higher law of *abstract principle*, but administered the lower law of *expediency*. In the *wilderness*, the law of *Brotherhood*—love thy neighbor as thyself—was declared and enforced. Their property and food (manna) was "*in common*" for forty years.

3. In Canaan, "*the land is mine*, saith the Lord; ye are stewards." *Six days* the people might buy and sell, and trade and traffic, and see who should get and keep the most. The *seventh day* was the Lord's, a sabbath to be kept by each one "*loving his neighbor as himself,*" the rich feeding and ministering to the wants of the poor—all rejoicing together before the Lord, and each other as brethren.

4. *Six months* also they had for *me and mine*. The *seventh* was a holy convocation, during which the higher law—*the law of love*—was the supreme law of the land. Again, *six years* were allotted for *selfhood* to develop itself, the legitimate fruit whereof brought forth debtor and creditor, and master and slave; and these relations were sustained and consummated. But the *seventh year* was the sabbatical year; and when the trumpet of this jubilee sounded, all debts were cancelled, and all slaves were restored to freedom. Equality of person was established, and the Lord reigned triumphant for one whole year.

5. All the spontaneous produce of the land was

free food for the Lord's people—the wheat, the grapes, the figs, etc., were gathered and eaten where they grew, by the poor and the fatherless, the widow and the orphan, the Levite and the stranger; and even the beasts of the field were not forgotten—they rested from their labors, and roamed the fields in peace.

6. The *fiftieth year* was the Sabbath of sabbaths, and there were concentrated in it all the equalizing elements and fraternal relations of the three preceding sabbaths; and, to crown the whole, the *land* itself, the foundation of all selfish property, was restored to its original and rightful owners. Thus the last grasp of the monopolizer and selfish speculator on the means of subsistence was loosened, and his selfish, unrighteous accumulations were divided and scattered; society became again resolved into its original elements, as in the wilderness, and a condition of *universal brotherhood* was established.

7. These four orders of sabbaths corresponded to the four Dispensations, or cycles. The last of them, the great Jubilee of jubilees, typified. in a

very perfect manner, the *sabbath of the world*, the fourth and last Dispensation, or cycle, wherein, *self* being destroyed, property is "common;" *lust* being crucified, a virgin life remains; the lion, *war*, being overcome by the lamb of *peace* and non-resistance, gentleness and tranquillity prevail; and, finally, the principle of *hate* being supplanted by love to God and man, we have the *non*-counterfeited seal of the second Christian Church.

8. In Jesus (as a perfect Jew) the promise of God through Moses, that he would "take all sickness away from the midst of thee," was fulfilled. This was the ultimate of the Mosaic Dispensation—to save the body from sickness, and "all the diseases of the Egyptians," or Gentiles, as perfectly as the Gospel of Jesus Christ will save the soul from all sin and spiritual infirmity.

9. Jesus was free from bodily disease; "and he went about doing good," by healing those Jews who were sick, lame, blind, or who had leprosy, or were possessed of demons. And when multitudes of invalids were brought to him, "he healed them all." This power he transmitted to his disciples,

and established it as one of the signs of a Christian, and of a Christian Church, saying, "These signs shall follow them that believe: they shall lay hands on the sick, and they shall be healed," etc.

PART II.

PROBATION, AND HEAVENS AND HELLS.

10. The four successive cycles into which the Shakers divide the religious history of mankind are not confined to this earth, but extend into, and are operative in, the spirit-world, where also a state of probation still continues, as upon this earth. Every human being that has ever existed upon this globe is within one or other of these cycles.

11. Each cycle has its appropriate heaven and hell—first, second, third, and fourth. No soul will be finally lost until it has rejected the greatest spiritual light of the fourth cycle.

12. The wicked antediluvians, who rejected the preaching of Noah, went to the *first hell;* the good went to the *first heaven*. The wicked Jews

go to the *second hell*, which Jews call *gehenna;* the righteous Jews, such as Abraham, Daniel, David, and others, went to the *second heaven*, which is called *Paradise*.

13. Paul was "caught up to the *third heaven*," that is, to the heaven of the cycle in which he lived, namely, the *third*, or first Christian Church. Jesus said, "No man hath ascended up to [the third] heaven but the Son of man, who is [already] in heaven." Even "David had not ascended into [the third] heaven."

14. Of the righteous within the *second* cycle, it is said, "These all died *in faith, not having received the promises*, God having provided some better thing for us, that *they without us* should not be made perfect." That is, the Jews out of the body, who had died hundreds of years before, would have the same Gospel of the kingdom preached to them that was preached to the inhabitants of Jerusalem who were then in the body.

15. Jesus himself did not ascend into the *fourth* heaven till after his departure from earth. He said to Mary, "Touch me not, for I am not yet

ascended," etc.; and again, it is said, "Jesus was not yet glorified."

16. Heaven or hell is first formed within every individual soul; then the law of affinity draws together, in the spirit-world, those whose states are homogeneous, and who internally are in the same heaven or hell, who happify or torment each other, as the case may be.

17. When Jesus had finished his work on earth—that is, organized a Church, and commissioned it to preach the Gospel to every creature in all nations—he "gave up the ghost," and "descended into hell"—the *first* hell—and preached the Gospel unto them who for many ages had been bound with chains of mental and spiritual darkness, and who were held by the cords of their own wicked and unbridled lusts, without either the knowledge, the will, or the power to break them; and he organized a Church, and commissioned those in it to freely give, as they had freely received.

18. "For this cause," said Peter, "was the Gospel preached to them that were dead, that they might be judged according to men in the flesh, but

live according to God, in the spirit." But, on his descent to this antediluvian hell, he must have passed through Paradise, the *second* heaven; for he said to the thief, "This day shalt thou be with me in Paradise."

19. When Jesus had laid the foundation for a Church among them, he ascended to his own proper sphere, or heaven. He informed his disciples that in his Father's house there were many mansions (or heavens) for them; that where he was, there they also might be.

20. In the Scriptures, mention is made of "heavens," and "heaven of heavens;" of the "new heavens;" and of the "old heavens passing away with a great noise;" of the "former heavens not being remembered, nor coming into mind any more;" and of "the powers of the heavens being shaken." These and kindred passages possess no meaning, except upon the principle that each cycle or Dispensation has its own heaven and hell, as before stated.

21. The heaven of the *fourth and last* Dispensation and Church is now in process of formation,

and will finally supersede the three previous heavens; for the principles, the ruling authority, and the governing "powers of these heavens," and the heavens themselves, will be "shaken," and "will pass away."

22. "The kingdom of heaven" of the *fourth* cycle is a state of purgation and final separation between the good and the evil, the true and the false. Souls in this kingdom are only "begotten of God," and they need to watch themselves, that they do not commit sin, and so fail of coming to the new birth.

23. But when souls are "born of God," they *can not* sin, for they have resisted temptation until their evil propensities and lusts are all destroyed, and the life of nature of the generative natural man is dead in them; as *Jesus* said of himself, before he left the body, "The prince of this world cometh, but hath nothing in me." He was born again.

24. This is a state that no other person could ever attain to, until Christ had made his second appearing, and the Mother Spirit was revealed;

for the man is not without the woman, nor the woman without the man, in the Lord, any more than in nature. And but few, while in the body, attain to the *new birth*, which is the end of the travail of the regeneration, the same as the birth of a natural infant is the end of the travail in generation. And as the *mother* is the bearing spirit with *natural* children, until they come to the natural birth, and begin to see and learn the things of the natural world, so also is the *spiritual* mother the bearing spirit, until the " new birth;" after which the spiritual child begins to learn the pure things of God on the highest and most spiritual plane. Then it is in the "heaven of heavens."

PART III.

GOD DUAL—FATHER AND MOTHER.

25. An all-important, sublime, and foundational doctrine of the Shakers is the Existence of an Eternal Father and an Eternal Mother in Deity— the Heavenly Parents of all angelical and human

beings. They claim that the *knowledge of God* has been *progressive*, from age to age, and from Dispensation to Dispensation.

26. In the *first* cycle, when spirituality in man was "as the waters to the ankles," God was known only as a great Spirit. In the *second* cycle, when spirituality was "as the waters to the knees," men began to inquire *who* and *what* God was, and received for answer, "I am that I am." You are not prepared to comprehend me further.

27. In the *third* cycle, when spirituality in the soul was "as the waters to the loins," God, for the first time, was revealed to man as *Father*.

28. And in the *fourth* cycle, when spirituality is becoming as a deep and broad expanse of waters, "that can not be measured" (see Ezek. xlvii.), God is also revealed in the character of *Mother*—an Eternal Mother—the bearing Spirit of all the creation of God, to whom the Shakers think reference is made in the Scriptures, particularly in the following extracts from the book of "Proverbs," under the appellation of *Wisdom:*

29. "The Lord possessed me in the beginning

of his way, before his works of old. I was set up from everlasting, from the beginning, or ever the earth was. When there were no depths I was brought forth: when there were no fountains abounding with water. Before the mountains were settled, before the hills was I brought forth: while as yet He had not made the earth, nor the fields, nor the highest part of the dust of the world.

30. "When He prepared the heavens, I was there: when He set a compass upon the face of the depth: when He established the clouds above: when He strengthened the fountains of the deep: when He gave to the sea his decree, that the waters should not pass his commandment: when He appointed the foundations of the earth: then I was by Him, as One brought up with Him; and I was daily his delight, rejoicing always before Him."

31. As *Father*, God is the infinite Fountain of intelligence, and the Source of all power—"the Almighty, great and terrible in majesty;" "the high and lofty One, that inhabiteth eternity, whose

name is Holy, dwelling in the high and holy place;" and "a consuming fire."

32. But, as *Mother*, "*God is love*" and tenderness! If all the *maternal* affections of all the female or bearing spirits in animated nature were combined together, and then concentred in *one individual human female*, that person would be but as a type or image of our Eternal Heavenly *Mother*.

33. The *duality* of God is expressed in the book of "Genesis" as follows: "Let us make man in our image, after our likeness. So God created man in his own image; male and female created He them; and called their name Adam."

34. From which, the Shakers insist, that it is the male and female in man that is peculiarly the "*image of God*." In this conclusion they further strengthen themselves from the Apostle Paul, who affirms that the order of the "Godhead," and the "eternal creative power of God," which would otherwise be invisible to man, are "clearly seen, by," through, and in, "the things that are made."

DOCTRINES OF THE CHURCH. 107

35. Consequently, if this be admitted, it follows, from the undeniable fact that all the things which God has "made" are *dual;* beginning with the *mineral* kingdom, which, from the "old red sandstone" to the very latest geological formation, exhibit the action of *two forces,* the positive and negative, which forms, in the *vegetable* kingdom, gradually resolve themselves into male and female types, from the fern to the polypus; and, in the *animal* kingdom, they are progressively developed from the polypus up to the simia tribes; and ultimately they culminate in *man* and *woman,* the image of God their Creator.

36. It seems scarcely possible to resist this evidence of a *dual order,* so "clearly seen" throughout all the domains of nature; or to admit it, without proving that *God also is* DUAL, Father and Mother, the image and likeness of man, whom He has made *male* and *female.*

37. "No carnal man hath seen God at any time," or witnessed an act of arbitrary, sovereign, creative power. The "eternal [creative] power" of God is only known to man through the per-

petual operation of the originating and reproducing powers of male and female principles.

38. The Shakers believe that the distinction of sex is eternal; that it inheres in the soul itself; and that no angels or spirits exist who are not male and female.

39. From the fact that Adam (and Eve) "was the figure of him that was to come," they argue that the "second Adam, the Lord from heaven, a quickening Spirit," was also *dual*, male and female; and that they were the spiritual Father and Mother of Jesus, begetting, watching over, and bearing him in the regeneration, towards the *new birth*, into their own quickening spiritual element.

40. Every thing is begotten, travails, and is born into the elements of its parents. "That which is [begotten and] born of the flesh, is flesh; and that which is [begotten and] born of the Spirit, is spirit."

41. Jesus, being a male, could only reveal and manifest the *Father* in Christ and God. But when the *second* Adam appeared to Ann, and became her spiritual Parents, she, being a female,

revealed and manifested the *Mother Spirit* in Christ and in Deity.

42. The affectional nature in man seeks its Source and Parent—the Maternal Spirit in Deity. Ignorance, or a perverted theology, may divert it into wrong channels, as in the worshipers of female gods in the heathen nations, which are known to be more numerous than all others; or the Roman Catholic adoration of the Virgin Mary—" the Mother of God." But nothing can destroy the intuitive reverence of the human soul for a *Heavenly Mother*. It is as innate and universal as is the belief in Deity.

43. From what has been said in the preceding pages, it will be readily inferred that the Shakers do not believe that God ever has appeared, or does now appear, to human beings, except through spiritual agencies. These have often personated Deity, and men have mistaken them for the Supreme Being; as in the case of John, who fell down to worship a being who proved to be one of his own brethren, the prophets; of Manoah and his wife, who thought they should die because they had seen

an angel, whom they mistook for God; and of Moses, who called the angel that appeared to him, and ministered the Law on Mount Sinai, God. Whereas the Apostle said, "The Law was ordained [ministered] by angels, in the hand of a mediator," Moses. And John declared that "no man had seen God at any time."

44. Christ was the highest and most purely spiritual being that ever visited the earth. All the preceding ministering spirits who spoke in the name of God (and that were "called gods, because," as Jesus said, "the word of God came to" and through "them"), in every cycle, were inferior to Christ, and to his order and sphere, being mediators between him and the earth's inhabitants in every nation.

45. Thus, previous to the *personal* appearing of Christ to Jesus and to Ann, he revealed himself through messengers—inferior spiritual agents, existing in the intermediate spheres of the spirit-world, earthward; and these revealed themselves to man, from sphere to sphere.

46. Hence it is said: "God, who at sundry

times, and in divers manners, spake to the fathers, *by the prophets* [in the spirit-world], hath, in these last days, spoken unto us by his Son." That is, the communication is *now more direct* than it was before; there are fewer intervening spheres and mediators between those who are in the *fourth* cycle and God.

47. Every cycle, or Dispensation, had its true Church, both in the spirit-world and on earth. These existed in a state of rapport with each other. The earth Church received its spiritual ministrations from the corresponding Church in the spirit-world. (See Heb. xii. 22 and 29.) It was the spiritual influx from that Church that was the Holy Ghost, or (as it ought to be rendered) Holy *Spirit;* for in the original languages the Holy Spirit is always designated by the neuter gender, *it.* It is the "anointing," blessing, or "unction," of the appointed lead in the *spirit* Church.

48. Every Church had its own Holy Spirit; and when it is said that "holy men of old wrote as they were moved by the Holy Ghost," it implies

that it was the Holy Spirit of *their Dispensation*, and of its Church in the spirit-sphere; which Holy Ghost would sanction and bless such things as were appropriate to that degree of the work of God, and to that cycle, or Dispensation.

49. Unless this idea of a *plurality* of Holy Spirits, as well as a plurality of cycles and Churches, be received and borne in mind, in reading the Scriptures, darkness and confusion of mind must ensue.

50. Jesus, in speaking of John the Baptist, said: "Of all that had been born of women, there had not arisen a greater than John," as a spiritual man, up to that time. "John was filled with the Holy Spirit from his mother's womb." If there were but *one* Holy Spirit, this would place John very high. But the fact is, John never became a Christian at all on earth; *he lived and died a Jew*. Consequently, John was not baptized with any higher spiritual influence than the Holy Spirit of the Jewish Church. And Jesus said, "He that is *least* in the kingdom of heaven, is *greater* than he"—*John*.

51. Jesus promised that, when he should come into the spirit-world, he would send his disciples the Comforter, or Holy Spirit. "In my Father's house are many mansions. I go to prepare a place for you." Jesus had first to establish the Church of the *third* Dispensation in the spirit-world, before he could send them *its* Holy Spirit, or that there could be a pentecostal day.

52. I will pray the Father, and He will give give you *another* Comforter, which is the Holy Spirit." Thus Jesus promised plainly to send them another Holy Ghost, distinct from any they had theretofore received, being the Holy Ghost of the *first* Christian Church.

53. The *second* Christian Church has also *its* Holy Spirit, and is the Church of the last Dispensation, or cycle. The Holy Spirit and influence proceeding from this Church in the spirit-world, is the *fire* with which John said Jesus would baptize souls; which fire will burn up the generative nature, while (at the same time) it is spiritual food, and creates souls anew in the resurrection, or regenerative state. Under its guidance, they seek

and find "those things that are above" the earthly order, where Jesus and Christ exist.

PART IV.

JUDGMENT DAY, AND CONFESSION OF SINS.

54. A radical and most important principle in the Shaker, or second Christian Church, is the *oral confession of sins to God*, in the presence of one or two witnesses.

55. This rests upon the premises that the natural man never has seen, and never will see, God personally, either in this or any other world. Therefore the judgment, as well as the mercy and goodness, of God, must necessarily be administered to souls through agencies appointed by a Divine revelation from God, for that express purpose, in all cycles and true Churches. This was the law and practice under the three preceding Dispensations, in the respective Churches thereof, while standing in rectitude.

56. The Mosaic Law said: "If a man sin, and

commit any of the things that are forbidden to be done, he shall confess that he hath sinned *in that thing ;* and he shall bring his trespass offering unto the Lord, for his sin which he hath sinned; and the priests shall make an atonement for him."

57. All those who came to John, and were baptized of water, did it "confessing their sins," as required by Moses. And even Jesus found his spiritual relation and union to John in the same order.

58. In founding Christianity, Jesus declared there was "nothing covered that should not be revealed; or hid that should not be made known." And, in ministering the Holy Spirit to the Apostles, after his crucifixion, he said: "Whosoever sins ye remit, they are remitted unto them; and whosoever sins ye retain, they are retained."

59. The *fallen Gentile* Christian Church having abused this institution, in common with every Christian doctrine, does not invalidate the principle itself, nor render it nugatory (in the proper order) in the true Church, but *confirms* it, as really as

does *counterfeit* coin *prove* that there is *true* money. Had there not been convincing evidence of *this principle* in the primitive Church, the Catholic priesthood could never have enforced its practice upon their votaries.

60. In the *second* appearing of Christ, the confession of sins was again restored and established in perfect order. Ann Lee confessed her sins to Jane and James Wardley; and she continually taught and enjoined it as the first act of a repentant soul, and as being absolutely essential to the reception of the *power to forsake sin*.

61. Mother Ann, and the elders with her, often revealed the most secret sins, that were purposely kept back by such as were opening their minds before them. Mother said: "The first step in obedience that any one of you can take, is to confess your sins to God, before his witnesses. Herein Christ is to be found as a Saviour, and a forgiver of sins, and nowhere else. For herein is contained the promise of God, but not in any other way."

62. Again, she said: "They that honestly con-

fess all their sins, with a full determination to forsake them forever, will find strength of God to forsake them; and in taking up the cross against every known sin, and following Christ in the regeneration, in that life of obedience, they will be clothed in the righteousness of Christ, and become the sons and daughters of God; being heirs of God, and joint-heirs with Jesus Christ."

63. At another time Mother said: "When I confessed my sins, I labored to remember the time when, and the place where, I committed them. And when I had confessed them, I cried to God to know if my confession was accepted; and by crying to God continually, I travelled out of my loss."

64. The experience of more than 70 years, by the Church, of the operation and effect of this principle (and practice) has well established it in the understanding, and confirmed it in the affections, of the people called Shakers.

PART V.

THE BIBLE.

65. The Shakers hold the Bible to be a record of the *most Divine* Angelic ministrations to man, and more or less an imperfect record of the spiritual and religious experience and history of the most highly progressed portion or branch of the human family.

66. They also believe that the state and condition of the seers, prophets, and prophetesses, or mediums, determined the quantity, and affected the quality, of every Divine revelation. The same may be said of the translators and translations of the Bible.

67. It is thought by the Shakers that the book of the "*Revelation*" has suffered less from interpolations and mistranslations than any other; partly by reason of the anathema it contains against all who should add to, or take from, its contents; but still more because the Spirit has clothed it with such a complexity of tropes, symbols, and figures, that it is utterly unintelligible to

the generative man, and could not be comprehended until the central event—the *second appearing of Christ*—had transpired; that being the only key by which to unlock its mysteries, break its seals, and unfold its treasures of wisdom and truth, by baptizing souls with the Spirit that dictated it, and forming in them the character of the "Lion of the tribe of Judah;" during which process, all the events described in *that book* would be accomplished in them as individuals. And, indeed, it is a chart of ecclesiastical history.

CHAPTER XI.

BIOGRAPHY OF THE SIX FOUNDERS OF THE SHAKER SOCIETY.

ANN LEE.

1. ANN LEE was born February 29, 1736, in Toad Lane (now Todd's Street), Manchester, England. Her father, John Lee, was a blacksmith; and, although poor, he was respectable in character, moral in principle, honest in his dealings, and industrious in his business. With him she resided until she embarked for America. Her mother was esteemed as a very pious woman. They had five sons and three daughters, who, as was then common for poor persons' children, were brought up to work, instead of being sent to school; by which means, Ann acquired an industrious habit, but could neither write nor read.

2. During her childhood and youth, she was em-

ployed in a cotton factory, and afterwards was a cutter of hatters' fur. She was also employed as cook in the Manchester infirmary, where she was distinguished for her neatness, faithfulness, prudence, and good economy.

3. In appearance, Ann Lee was about the common stature of women. She was thick-set, but straight, well-proportioned, and regular in form and features. Her complexion was light and fair, blue eyes, and light chesnut brown hair. Her countenance was mild and expressive, but grave and solemn. Her glance was keen and penetrating; her countenance inspired confidence and respect. Many called her beautiful.

4. She possessed a sound, strong, and healthy physical constitution, and remarkable powers and faculties of mind. At times, when under the operation of the Holy Spirit, her form and actions appeared to be divinely beautiful and angelic. The power and influence of her spirit was then beyond description, and she spoke as "one having authority."

5. In childhood, she exhibited a bright, saga-

cious, and active genius. She was not addicted to play, like other children of her age, but was serious and thoughtful. She was early the subject of religious impressions, and was often favored with heavenly visions.

6. As she advanced in years she was strongly impressed with a sense of the deep depravity of human nature, and of the odiousness of sin, especially the impure and indecent nature of sexual coition for mere gratification. To her mother she often expressed her feelings respecting these things, and earnestly desired to be kept and preserved from sin, and from those abominations her soul so much abhorred.

7. But, notwithstanding her repugnance to the marriage state, through the importunities of her relations, she was induced to be married to Abraham Stanley, a blacksmith, by whom she had four children, who died in their infancy.

8. She continued to reside at her father's house; but the convictions of her youth often returned upon her with much force, which at length brought her under excessive tribulation of soul, in which

she sought earnestly for deliverance from the bondage of sin, and gave herself no rest, day or night, but often spent whole nights in laboring and crying to God to open some way of salvation.

9. In the year 1758, and 23d year of her age, she united herself to a society called *Shakers* which was under the ministration of Jane and James Wardley, formerly of the Quaker order. The people of that society were of blameless deportment, and were distinguished for the clearness and swiftness of their testimony against sin, the strictness of their moral discipline, and for the purity of their lives.

10. The light of this people led them to an open confession of every sin they had committed, and to take up a full and final cross against everything they knew to be evil. This endowed them with great power over sin; and here Ann found that protection she had so long desired, and which corresponded with her faith at that time. She was baptized into the same Spirit, and by degrees travelled to the full knowledge and experience of all the spiritual truths of the Society.

11. To her followers she said: "I love the day that I first received the Gospel. I call it my birthday. I cried to God, without intermission, for three days and three nights, that He would give me *true desires*. And when I received a gift of God, I did not go away and forget it, and travel no further; but I stood faithful, day and night, warring against all sin, and praying to God for deliverance from the *very nature of sin*. And other persons need not expect to find power over sin without the same labor and travel of soul.

12. "I felt such a sense of my sins that I was willing to confess them before the whole world. I confessed my sins to my elders, one by one, and repented of them in the same manner. When my elders reproved me, I felt determined not to be reproved twice for the same thing, but to labor to overcome the evil for myself.

13. "Soon after I set out to travel in the way of God, I labored a-nights in the work of God. Sometimes I labored all night, continually crying to God for my own redemption. Sometimes I went to bed and slept; but in the morning, if I

could not feel that sense of the work of God that I did before I slept, I would labor all night. This I did many nights, and in the daytime I put my hands to work, and my heart to God; and when I felt weary and in need of rest, I labored for the power of God, and the refreshing operations thereof would release me, so that I felt able to go to my work again.

14. "Many times, when I was about my work, I have felt my soul overwhelmed with sorrow. I used to work as long as I could keep it concealed, and then would go out of sight, lest any one should pity me with that pity which was not of God. In my travel and tribulation my sufferings were so great, that my flesh consumed upon my bones, bloody sweat pressed through the pores of my skin, and I became as helpless as an infant. And when I was brought through, and born into the spiritual kingdom, I was like an infant just born into the natural world. They see colors and objects, but they know not what they see. It was so with me; but before I was 24 hours old, I saw, and I knew what I saw."

15. Ann was wrought upon after this manner for the space of nine years. Yet she often had intervals of releasement, in which her bodily strength and vigor was sometimes miraculously renewed; and, at times, her soul was filled with heavenly visions and Divine revelations. By these means the way of God and the nature of his work gradually opened upon her mind with increasing light and understanding.

16. The Divine manifestations she received from time to time were communicated to the Society, and tended greatly to enlighten the minds and strengthen the faith of the members, and to increase and confirm the testimony. Her mind, ever intent upon the great work of salvation, was greatly affected concerning the lost state of mankind. But the real foundation of that loss was still concealed from her view; nor could she see any prospect of recovery under the existing circumstances; for she had long been convinced that there was nothing in all the professions and practices of professors that could save them from sin here, or furnish to them any reasonable hope of salvation hereafter.

17. She spent much time in earnest and incessant cries to God, to show her the foundation of man's loss, what it was, and wherein it consisted; and how the way of salvation could be discovered and effectually opened to mankind in the state they were then in, and how the great work of redemption was to be accomplished.

18. The ultimate fruit of the labor and suffering of soul that Ann passed through was to purify and fitly prepare her for becoming a temple in whom the same Christ Spirit that had made a *first* appearing to Jesus, at his baptism by John in Jordan (the river of Judgment), at which time he received the anointing which constituted him Jesus Christ, could make a *second* appearing; and through whom the God of heaven could set up a Church, or "kingdom, which should never be destroyed;" for all previous Churches had been destroyed by and through the operation of the fleshly lusts of their own members. They all commenced in the Spirit, and with a cross; but, through self-indulgence, "ended in the flesh."

19. While Ann, for her testimony against

"fleshly lusts, which war against the soul," was imprisoned in Manchester, England, she saw Jesus Christ in open vision, who revealed to her the most astonishing views and Divine manifestations of truth, in which she had a perfect and clear sight of the "mystery of iniquity," the root and foundation of all human depravity, and of the very act of transgression committed by Adam and Eve in the garden of Eden.

20. Thus it was made plain to her understanding how and in what manner all mankind were lost from God, and that a complete cross against the *lusts of generation*, added to a full and explicit confession, before witnesses, of all the sins committed under its influence, was the only possible effectual remedy and means of salvation; and also that absolute death to the generative or propagative life itself (in even its most innocent, uncorrupted state), was the preliminary step to the quickening and resurrection of the hidden spiritual life of God in the soul, which life is eternal in its nature and duration.

21. Does not this disclose the meaning of the

Scripture phrase, "the Lamb slain from," cut off and elevated above, "the foundation" principle "of the" natural "world?" which is the life of the innocent generative nature of man operating upon the procreative or propagative animal plane, that from the beginning was designed to be merely temporary—a stepping-stone to a superior order, as the worm state to that of the butterfly. And, after having subserved its *use* of producing and continuing the race, to be slain, and then supplanted by the opening of the next discrete degree —the Divine-spiritual—in the soul, which is the ultimate and final resurrection.

22. The foregoing is agreeable to the Scripture records, and is a fulfillment of the prophetic sayings in · the books of the "Revelation" and "Psalms" —"The marriage of the Lamb is come, and his wife hath *made herself ready*." "She is arrayed in fine linen, clean and white; for the fine linen is the righteousness of saints." The King and Queen mentioned in the forty-fifth Psalm do evidently show forth the *dual* order of the kingdom of Christ. No one disputes that the King

refers to Jesus; but *who* is the *Queen* that stood at his right hand, adorned with gold of Ophir? to whom the Spirit saith, "Forget also thine *own people*, and thy *father's house;* so shall the King greatly desire thy beauty; for he is thy Lord, and worship thou him."

23. "She is all glorious *within!* her clothing is of wrought gold and fine needlework," very labored: all going to show that she had a great work to do, to fit her for the spiritual order, and to "make herself ready."

24. The "virgins, her companions, that follow her," are the men and women who constitute the virgin Church. "They are brought with gladness and rejoicing to the King's palace." And the name of the Queen would be "remembered through all generations; and the people would praise her forever."

25. And, "instead of her father's, should be *her* children, whom she would make princes in all the earth;" being the spiritual posterity of the "King and Queen." All this is being literally accomplished in the Church of Christ's Second Appearing.

26. From the time of the appearing of Christ to Ann, in the prison, she was received by the people as a Mother in spiritual things, and was thenceforth by them called *Mother Ann*.

27. The exercises in their religious assemblies were singing and dancing, shaking and shouting, speaking with new tongues, and prophesying, with all those various gifts of the Holy Spirit known in the Primitive Church. These gifts progressively increased until the time of the full establishment of the Church in America.

28. From that time (1770) Mother Ann, by the immediate revelation of Christ, bore an open testimony against all lustful gratifications, as the source and foundation of human corruption and misery. She testified in the most plain and pointed manner that no soul could follow Christ in the regeneration, while living in the works of natural generation.

29. Her testimony was often delivered with such mighty spiritual power, accompanied with so heart-searching and soul-quickening a spirit, that it seemed to penetrate every secret of the heart. But, to those who rejected her testimony, it often

had the effect of arousing in them the most bitter and relentless spirit of persecution, more especially among high professors in the popular churches, in which the lusts of the world and religion were and are combined.

30. The ministration of power over all sin, attended with visions, revelations, and other spiritual gifts, was the *seal* of Mother Ann's testimony to those who received it.

31. The immediate cause, or pretense, of the imprisonment already referred to, was dancing, shouting, shaking, etc., in the worship of God, on the Sabbath day—"*Sabbath breaking.*"

32. These meetings excited public attention, and stirred up the malignant feelings of many, both professors (especially of the clergy) and profane, of almost every class and description, to such a degree of enmity, that, by formal opposition and tumultuous mobs, open persecution and secret malice, the life of *Ann* was many times in great jeopardy.

33. She was often shamefully and cruelly abused, and several times imprisoned. She was once drag-

ged out of the meeting by a mob, and cast into a prison in Manchester. They put her in a cell so small that she could not straighten herself, and, with the design of starving her to death, kept her there fourteen days without food; nor was the door opened during all that time. She had nothing to eat or drink, except some wine and milk mixed, put into the bowl of a tobacco-pipe, and conveyed to her by inserting the stem through the key-hole once every 24 hours. This was done by James Whittaker, when a boy, whom Mother Ann brought up. When taken out of prison, her enemies were astonished to see her walk off, looking as well as when she entered.

34. "On another occasion," she said, "a great mob came against me, determined to put an end to my existence. They took me into the high road, and ordered me to advance. In submission thereto, I made the attempt, but was soon knocked down with clubs; and after I got up and began to walk, I was kicked every few steps for two miles. I then felt almost ready to give up the ghost, and was faint with thirst. While I was suffering by the

merciless mob, not one friend was allowed to follow me. But God in his mercy remembered me, and sent a deliverer.

35. "A certain nobleman living some distance, who knew nothing of what was passing, was remarkably wrought upon in his mind, and urged by his feelings to go; but where, or for what cause, he did not know. He ordered his servant to fetch his horse immediately. The servant went in haste, but the nobleman's anxiety was so great that he sent a messenger after his servant to hasten him. Having mounted his horse, he rode as if it had been to save his own life, as he afterwards told me. He came to a large concourse of persons, and on being informed what their business was, he rode up to the place where I was, and sharply reproved the mob for their abuse and cruel conduct, and dispersed them, and I was restored to my friends."

36. Mother Ann was repeatedly delivered from imminent danger by the same invisible power that induced this nobleman to release her. At one time a mob attempted to bind her with ropes, but were

unable to do so by reason of the spiritual power by which she was exercised.

37. At another time she was accused of *blasphemy*, and was told that her tongue should be bored through with a hot iron, and her cheek branded. She was brought before four ministers of the Established Church, with a view to obtain judgment against her. They asked her to speak in other tongues, but she told them that unless she should feel the power of God she could not do that. She was soon operated upon, and spoke for four hours of the wonderful works of God.

38. These *clergymen* were great linguists, and they testified that she had spoken in seventy-two different tongues. This had the effect of causing them to advise the mob not to molest her, which only disappointed and enraged them, and they resolved themselves into her judges and executioners, and decided to stone her to death as a *blasphemer*.

39. The mob then took Mother Ann, William Lee, and James and Daniel Whittaker into a valley outside the town; and having provided them-

selves with stones suitable in size and number, they threw them at their victims, but could not hit either of them. They then fell into contention among themselves, and abandoned their wicked design.

40. Mother Ann said: "While they were throwing the stones I felt myself surrounded by the presence of God, and my soul was filled with love. I knew they could not kill me, for my work was not done; therefore I felt joyful and comfortable, while my enemies felt confusion and distress."

41. Mother Ann related an instance of persecution she received from one of her brothers thus:— "One of my brothers, being greatly enraged, said he was determined to overcome me; so he brought a staff about the size of a broom-handle, and came to me as I was sitting in a chair, singing by the power of God. He beat me over the face and nose with the staff, till one end of it was much splintered. I sensibly felt and saw the bright rays of the glory of God pass between my face and the staff, and I did but just feel the blows. He continued beating until he was so far spent that he called for drink. He then began again with the

other end of the staff, and I felt my breath like healing balsam, which healed me, so that I felt no harm from the strokes."

42. "At another time [she said], in the evening, I was informed by a friend that there was a mob after me. I ran out to the back side of a hill, where there was a pond covered with ice. I laid down upon the ice, and remained there all night, in great peace and consolation, and did not take cold." These were but a small part of the persecutions suffered by Mother Ann.

43. On one occasion a man started from Manchester to go to the king, to obtain a license to banish Mother Ann and her followers from the country; but on the way he died, as was believed, by a judgment of God. Some others of their bitter persecutors met with untimely deaths in an unusual manner; others of them were deeply convicted; and fear fell upon the remainder.

44. For two years previous to their leaving England, persecution entirely ceased, and they enjoyed their faith in peace, and worshiped God unmolested.

45. On the 19th of May, 1774, Mother Ann, Abraham Stanley (her husband), William Lee, James Whittaker, John Hocknell, Richard Hocknell, James Shepherd, Mary Partington, and Nancy Lee embarked for America, in the ship Mariah, Captain Smith, of New York. All of them had received spiritual manifestations, and the Spirits directed them to repair to America, and informed them that the Church of Christ's Second Appearing would be established in that country.

46. Mother Ann said: "I knew by the revelation of God, that God had a chosen people in America; I saw some of them in vision; and when I met with them in America, I knew them. I had a vision of America: I saw a large tree, every leaf of which shone with such brightness as made it appear like a burning torch, representing the Church of Christ, which will yet be established in this land.

47. "Previous to our coming we called a meeting, and there were so many gifts (such as prophecies, revelations, visions, and dreams) in confirmation

of a former revelation for us to come, that some could hardly wait for others to tell their gifts. We had a joyful meeting, and danced till morning."

48. James Whittaker, one of Mother Ann's companions and followers, said: "Before we embarked, Mother Ann told the captain that he should not have whereof to accuse us, except it were concerning the law of our God. And when we went forth to praise God in songs and dances, the captain was greatly offended, and threatened to throw us overboard if we repeated the offence.

49. "But we, believing it better to obey God rather than man, when we felt a gift of God, again went forth in the same manner to worship Him, trusting in Him for protection. This so greatly enraged the captain, that he attempted to put his threat into execution.

50. "This was in the time of a storm, and the vessel sprang a leak, occasioned by the starting of a plank; and the water flowed in so rapidly, that, although all the pumps were put into use, it gained upon us very fast. The whole crew were greatly alarmed, and the captain turned as pale

as a corpse, and said all would perish before morning.

51. "But Mother maintained her confidence in God, and said, 'Captain, be of good cheer; there shall not a hair of our heads perish; we shall arrive safe in America. I just saw two bright angels of God standing by the mast, through whom I received this promise.' She then encouraged the seamen, and she and her companions assisted at the pumps, when there came a great wave, which struck the ship with such violence that the plank was forced into its place, and all were soon released from the pumps.

52. "After this, the captain gave us full liberty to worship God according to the dictates of our own consciences, and promised never to molest us again, and during the remainder of the voyage we were treated with kindness. In New York, the captain declared that, if it had not been for these people, he should never have reached America."

53. Having landed in New York (August 6, 1774), the company had to divide, to seek employ-

ment in different directions; for, being poor, manual labor was their only means of subsistence.

54. Mother Ann remained in New York; and the connection between her and Abraham Stanley was soon after dissolved by the latter marrying another woman; shortly after which, Mother Ann went up the river to Albany, and from thence to Niskeuna, (a wilderness, but) now Watervliet. Here the company was reunited, and remained very secluded for about three years and a half.

55. In the spring of 1780, the converts of a very remarkable religious revival at New Lebanon, N. Y., began to visit them, many of whom united with them; and thus the material was prepared for a Shaker Society at that place. Consequent upon this addition to their number, opposition and persecution were excited; and, as the revolutionary war was then in progress, some designing men accused them of being *unfriendly to the patriotic cause*, from the fact of their bearing a testimony against *war in general*.

56. They were arraigned before the commissioners of Albany, under the above charge, and were

required to purge themselves from the suspicion of being enemies in disguise, by taking the oath of allegiance. But swearing was also contrary to their faith.

57. Whereupon David Darrow, Joseph Meacham, and John Hocknell were put into prison; then Hezekiah Hammond and Joel Pratt; and, finally, Mother Ann, Mary Partington, Wm. Lee, James Whittaker, and Calvin Harlow were also imprisoned in Albany, in July of this year.

58. These were the leaders and elders of the people. They were treated with kindness by the commissioners; and many sensible, candid persons expressed their displeasure at the injustice and inconsistency of imprisoning an innocent, harmless people for their religious faith, while the country itself was struggling for freedom of person and liberty of conscience.

59. The elders were much visited in prison, and many received faith in the people and their principles, and came and confessed their sins, and *"showed their deeds."* Such, indeed, was the power of God that accompanied the word and testi-

mony, that often some in the crowd were seized with conviction; and open confession of every known sin was made through the grating of the prison, so mightily grew the Word of God, and prevailed. Thus, unwittingly, their persecutors took the most effectual means to spread the very work they aimed to suppress.

60. Believers were allowed the privilege of communing with them in prison, and administered to their necessities. Mother Ann, however, was soon separated from the company, and, accompanied by Mary Partington, was conveyed down the river, with the intention of banishing her to the British army; but, providentially failing in that, she was lodged in the jail at Poughkeepsie.

61. Near the close of the same year, the elders in Albany were released from prison, without any trial, *by order of Governor George Clinton*, after being confined six months, without any cause, except their religious faith. And being informed by those released of the imprisonment of Mother Ann at Poughkeepsie, he released her also. This was in December, 1780, when she joyfully returned to

her spiritual children, to their great comfort and consolation.

62. In May, 1781, Mother Ann and the elders left Watervliet, on a missionary journey to Harvard, Mass., and other places in the Eastern States, and did not return until 1783, having been absent two years and four months. During this journey many persons, in different places, received the Gospel and became joined to them.

63. Again they were subjected to the most bitter and violent persecutions. They were whipped, beaten with clubs, stoned, kicked, dragged about by their legs and arms, and sometimes by the hair of their heads; and they were driven from place to place in the most cruel and abusive manner, so that many of them narrowly escaped with their lives, and numbers of them carried through life the marks and scars of the wounds which they had received from their inhuman persecutors. Through all these trying scenes they were evidently protected and supported by the power and providence of God, so that no life was suffered to be taken.

64. Some singular and dreadful judgments fol-

lowed the prominent actors in those persecutions; and it became a proverb among the world: "These Shaker drivers are all coming to nought;" and the persecutions finally altogether ceased, but were the effectual means of spreading the faith and increasing the number of the believers in the second appearing of Christ.

65. Mother Ann, having finished her work on earth, departed this life, at Watervliet, on the 8th day of September, 1784, aged 48 years and six months.

66. [Christopher Love (who was beheaded under Cromwell) prophesied that "Out of thee, O England, shall a bright star arise, whose light and voice shall make *the heavens* quake and knock under with submission to the blessed Jesus." To whom could this apply, if not to the Divine light and work of Mother Ann?]

67. Mother Ann, being inquired of, by Joseph Meacham, as to how it was that she, being a woman, *taught* in the Church, and was even the Head of it, replied: "The order of God in the natural creation is a figure of the order of God in the spiritual creation.

68. "As in nature it requires a man and a woman to produce children, the man is first and the woman second in the government of the family; he is the father, and she the mother; and the male and female children must be subject to their parents, and the woman subject to her husband, who is the *first;* and when the man is gone, the right of government does not belong to the children, but to the *woman:* so *is the family of Christ.*"

69. Temporal economy she inculcated thus: "You must be prudent and saving of every good thing that God blesses you with, that you may have to give to the needy. You could not make either a kernel of grain or a spear of grass grow, if you knew you must die for the want of it."

70. "The Gospel [she said] is the greatest treasure that souls can possess. Be faithful; put your hands to work and your hearts to God. Beware of covetousness, which is as the sin of witchcraft. If you have anything to spare, give it to the poor."

71. At another time, in addressing a company

of Believers, she said: "It is now spring of the year, and you have all had the privilege of being taught the way of God; now you may all go home, and be faithful with your hands. Every faithful man will go and put up his fences in season, and will plow his ground in season, and will put his crops into the ground in season. Such a man may with confidence look for a blessing.

72. "But the slothful and indolent will say: *To-morrow will do as well, and to-morrow will do as well.* Such a man never finds a blessing; or, if he get anything, it is *afterwards*, and there seems to be no blessing in it. Just so he is in spiritual things. He will be slothful in the work of God, and will reap his reward. He that is unfaithful in the unrighteous mammon, how can he be trusted with the true riches?"

73. To a sister she said: "Be faithful to keep the Gospel; be neat and industrious; keep your family's clothes clean and decent. See that your house is kept clean, and your victuals prepared in good order; that when the brethren come home from their hard work, they may bless you, and eat

their food with thankfulness, without murmuring, and be able to worship God in the beauty of holiness. Watch, and be careful; don't speak harshly, nor cast reflections upon them. Let your words be few, and seasoned with grace."

74. To another sister she said: "You must remember the poor and needy, the widow and the fatherless; and deal out your bread to the hungry, and your clothes to the naked. Your *natures* will say, They may work, and get these things for themselves. But *Christ* said, '*Give to him that asketh.*'

75. "You must put away your covetousness, your lust, and your filthiness, and be prepared for the increase of the Gospel. For the time will come when this Gospel will be preached to all nations, and many will flock to Zion to hear the Word of the Lord. Remember the cries of those who are in need and trouble, that when you are in trouble God may hear your cries."

76. To other sisters she said: "Little children are innocent, and they should never be brought out of it. If brought up in simplicity, they would

receive good as easy as evil. Do not blame them for every little fault. Teach them obedience; let your word be law. Never speak to them in a passion; it will put devils into them. When I was a child my mind was taken up with things of God, so that I saw heavenly visions instead of trifling toys. Do all your work as though you had a thousand years to live, and as though you were going to die to-morrow."

77. Of herself, Mother Ann said: "Once my feet walked in forbidden paths; my hands handled unclean things; and my eyes saw nothing of God aright. Now my eyes see, my ears hear, and my hands handle the Word of life." To some she said: "You never can enter the kingdom of God with hard feelings against any one. For God is love; and if you love God, you will love one another."

78. In addressing an assembly of Believers, at Watervliet, shortly after her return from Poughkeepsie, she spoke as follows: "You are called in relation to all the rest of mankind; and through your faith and obedience they must receive the

Gospel. Pain and sufferings will never cease in the Church until all souls have heard the Gospel of salvation; for this Gospel will be freely offered to all souls, and will be the savor of life unto life, or of death unto death.

79. "The increase of the Gospel, at first, will be small; but the time will come when souls will embrace it by hundreds and by thousands; for this testimony will overcome all nations. It will increase till the covering is taken off; then mankind will see the rottenness of antichrist's foundation; then those souls that are bound in their sins will call to the rocks and to the mountains to cover them. But the saints will never be overcome again by the beastly power of antichrist.

80. "The work of God, in this day, is an inward, spiritual work. It is not so great in *outward* appearance as it was in past Dispensations; therefore souls must be very cautious how they treat this Gospel. For such as finally reject the testimony thereof in this world, will not have another day" equal to this; nor until an offer of the Gospel shall have been made to the entire race of Adam.

81. Those who obey the Gospel on earth, taking up their cross as Jesus did, "stand with him on Mount Zion," being of "the hundred and forty-four thousand:" these are in the first resurrection; while those who receive and obey the Gospel in their disembodied state constitute the second fruits. This class is thus noticed by the Revelator (Rev. vii. 9): "After this, I beheld, and lo, a great multitude, which no man could number, of all nations, and kindreds, and people, and tongues, stood before the throne, and before the Lamb, clothed with white robes [righteousness], and palms [victories they had gained] in their hands."

82. These "cried, with a loud voice, Salvation to our God." And the question being asked, "What are these which are arrayed in white robes? and whence came they?" the answer was: "These are they which came out of great tribulation, and have washed their robes, and made them white in the blood [or by living the life] of the Lamb" in the spirit-world.

83. Mother Ann said: "All souls will have an offer of the Gospel in this world, or in the world

of spirits." And she added: "You have your day now. You can, by obedience, travel out of your loss, by taking up the cross that Jesus did. But souls in the world of spirits have to travel through sufferings, passing from prison to prison, until they find the mercy of God."

84. Disembodied souls are saved through sufferings, and by the labors of the "kings and priests unto God and the Lamb," who had followed the example of Jesus in the earth-life. And as Jesus "preached to the spirits in prison," so such, like him, are "baptized for the dead." (See 1 Cor. xv. 29.)

85. Mother Ann also said: "Those who voluntarily take up their crosses in *this* world, and faithfully endure to the end, will be more bright and glorious than any others. They will be the 'kings and priests unto God.'"

86. On a certain occasion she said: "Put not your trust in any man or woman, but in the power and gift of God." Again, she said: "The room over your head is full of angels of God. I see them; and you could see them if you were re-

deemed. I look in at the windows of heaven, and see what there is the invisible world. I see the angels of God, and hear them sing. I see the glories of God. I see Ezekiel Goodrich flying from one heaven to another." And, turning to the company present, she said, "Go in, and join his resurrection." She then began to sing, and they praised the Lord in the dance.

87. On another occasion she said: "The Apostles, in their day, saw as through a glass darkly; but we see face to face, and see things as they are, and converse with spirits, and see their states. The Gospel is preached to souls who have left the body. I see thousands of the dead rising, and coming to judgment, now, at this present time."

88. She also said: "If there be but one called of a generation, and that soul be faithful, it will have to travel and bear for all its generation; for the world will be redeemed by generations." She saw disembodied souls laboring for the power of God, and said that such were in a travail.

89. One morning she said: "Last night I was under sufferings. A great number of the dead

came to me. Some of them embraced the Gospel; others chose rather to go to hell than confess their sins. I have seen, in vision, beautiful souls of men arrayed in white, all in the resurrection. There is no fear of their going back. As for hell, they have had enough of it; and come back again into this world they can not. But poor man in the body is always in danger.

90. "I have seen Jane in the world of spirits, praising God in the dance. I have seen young Jonathan Wood among the dead; he was like claps of thunder among them, waking them up. I have been all night with the dead. I heard the archangel sound the trumpet, and I heard Ezekiel's voice roar from one prison to another, preaching to the dead; and they gather to him, and are thankful to hear the Word of God. [This was soon after the decease of Ezekiel Goodrich.] And if you do not receive the Word of God which is spoken to you, the dead will; for there is not one word of God lost that ever was spoken."

91. Speaking of a particular person who had deceased, Mother Ann said: "Since that time he

has appeared to me again, and has arisen from the dead, and come into the first heaven, and is travelling on to the second and third heavens."

92. When any person knelt down to Mother Ann, she would say to them: "Do not kneel to me; kneel to God. I am but your fellow-servant."

93. Believers were not gathered into the order of community of goods during the lifetime of Mother Ann. She said: "The time will come when the Church will be gathered into order, but not till after my decease. Joseph Meacham is my first-born son in America: he will gather the Church into order, but I shall not live to see it."

CHAPTER XII.

WILLIAM LEE.

1. **WILLIAM LEE** was the fourth son of John Lee, and the brother of Ann Lee. He was born in the year 1740, in Manchester, England. By trade he was a blacksmith. He came to America with his sister Ann. He possessed uncommon physical strength and fortitude of mind. In his religious faith and practice he was zealous and influential, and in times of persecution always firm and undaunted. He knew not the fear of man.

2. He was married, and was an officer in the army—the Oxford Blues—previous to joining his sister Ann in her new system of religion. He described himself as having been a very proud, haughty young man, fond of dress and gaiety.

But, under the influence of his religious convictions, he forsook all, to be a follower of his sister Ann, and to her he was an invaluable assistant and protector; the scars from wounds received in her defence he carried to his grave.

3. At one time his skull was fractured by a blow from an iron boat-hook. Indeed, his sufferings of body and soul for the Gospel cause, as preached and lived by Mother Ann, were such that his companions said that, "like Jesus, he was a man of sorrows, and acquainted with grief."

4. He was richly endowed with spiritual gifts of visions and revelations, and many divine manifestations; he abounded in mercy, love, and charity, and his powerful spirit always maintained a swift testimony against all sin.

5. He possessed a great degree of thankfulness for common blessings. At one time he said: "I fear you are not so thankful as you ought to be for the good things that God has provided for you; but you eat and drink of these precious things without considering from whence they come. The sin of ingratitude is a great sin—see that you are

not guilty of it. I often eat my food with thankfulness and tears every mouthful I eat." He manifested the same thankful spirit even for water, whether to drink, or for any other use.

6. To the brethren and sisters he said: "You ought to pass each other like angels. I know the condition of souls that have left the body. Where I see one soul in the body, I see a thousand in the world of spirits."

7. He said: "War will never cease until God has finished His work with the nations of the earth. And, although it may be buried for a season, yet, like fire, it will break out with sevenfold increase among the nations of the earth. The same sword that has persecuted the people of God in past ages will be turned into the world among themselves, and it will never be sheathed till it has done its work."

8. "We are poor [said he], but we are able to make many rich: poor afflicted people of God. Once I served God out of fear, but now I serve Him out of love. I love my Mother. Although she is my sister, yet she has become my

Mother, and the Lord God has made me to love her."

9. The gift of songs was peculiarly his, and he had a melodious and powerful voice, and was a beautiful and musical singer. He deceased July 21st, 1784, aged 44 years.

CHAPTER XIII.

JAMES WHITTAKER.

1. JAMES WHITTAKER was the son of Jonathan Whittaker. His mother's maiden name was Ann Lee—probably a distant relation of Mother Ann. They were members of the Society under Jane and James Wardley, and subsequently embraced the Gospel. His father had an anxious feeling to come to America with Mother Ann, but was not able. He died in the faith.

2. James was born February 28th, 1751, in Oldham, near Manchester, England. He received the testimony of the Gospel in his childhood, and used to accompany his parents to the meetings of Jane and James Wardley, and was faithful and obedient to the instructions of his teachers. In his youth he was placed under the care of Mother Ann, and by her was carefully instructed in the

way of God. Having, by his faithfulness, gained a great portion of the light and power of the Gospel, he became eminently useful to her in the ministry.

3. Concerning his early experience in the way of God, he gave the following particulars: "I was brought up in the way of God by my Mother [Ann], and I knew no unclean thing. Yet, when my soul was waked up, I found myself a child of wrath. I then cried mightily to God. I do not think I spoke more than five words in a day; and I verily thought the earth trembled under me for the space of a whole year. At this time I saw, by vision, my own soul with Mother's in America, and I heard all the conversation that passed between us and the men that put us into prison in Albany; and yet, during the whole time of my imprisonment, I never once thought of my vision; but as soon as we were set at liberty, it all came fresh to my mind."

4. Among other extraordinary manifestations of God to him, in early life, are the two following, in his own words: "One day, as I was walking with

Mother, I felt the heavens open; such flows of the heavenly manifestations and givings of God fell upon me in so marvelous a manner, that my soul was filled with inexpressible glory; and I felt such an overflowing of love to Mother, that I cried out, As the Lord liveth, and as my soul liveth, I will never leave thee nor forsake thee." He added further: "Mother then and there prophesied that I should succeed her in the ministry."

5. He said: "When we were in England, some of us had to go twenty miles to meeting. We travelled a-nights, on account of the persecution. One Saturday night, while on our journey, we sat down by the side of the road to eat some victuals. While I was sitting there I saw a vision of America; and I saw a large tree, every leaf of which shone with such brightness as made it appear like a burning torch, representing the Church of Christ which will yet be established in this land. After my company had refreshed themselves, they travelled on, and led me a considerable distance before my vision ceased."

6. In his person, James was rather above the

common stature, well proportioned in form, of more than ordinary strength, and of great activity. His complexion was fair, his eyes black, and his hair was dark brown, and very straight. His countenance was open and placid, with a pleasing gravity that evinced the goodness of his heart, and the amiable mildness of his disposition. His voice was clear and solid, but mild and pleasant. In short, his visage, deportment, and conversation were all marked with an inexpressible quality, which could not but impress the feelings of a stranger with confidence and respect. It was not uncommon among strangers, on hearing him, to say, "I love to hear that James Whittaker speak."

7. In his temper and disposition he was mild, gentle, and forbearing, yet firm, undaunted, and inflexible in his duty. So amiable was his deportment, and so winning his manners, that he often disarmed the most violent opposers of their rage. He possessed much meekness, humility, and simplicity of soul; he was tender-hearted, kind, and charitable, and abounded in heavenly love. The

sympathetic powers of his soul were such that, when he wept, it seemed as though no feeling heart could refrain from tears; and when he rejoiced, every soul that possessed the life of the Gospel could not but feel the power of his joy, and rejoice with him.

8. In reproving sin he was sharp and powerful, yet wise and careful not to hurt the soul. In laboring with souls, in admonishing the careless, instructing the ignorant, strengthening the weak, and binding up the broken-hearted, he evidenced much wisdom. He knew how to come to souls in every situation, and to administer help in due season.

9. He passed through many scenes of sorrow and affliction for the Gospel of salvation, and planted and nourished it in many souls. Being young while in England, he did not suffer so much persecution there as did Mother Ann and Father William and others; yet he had his full share of sufferings to pass through, so that it might be truly said, *the sufferings of Christ abounded in him.*

10. In America he suffered much every way;

yet he always bore his sufferings with fortitude, and even with cheerfulness; so that, when most cruelly abused by persecutors, he would often kneel down and pray for them with great fervency, sometimes in the words of Christ, saying, "Father, forgive them, for they know not what they do."

11. As he was brought up in the Gospel from his childhood, he possessed a great degree of purity of spirit. Indeed, it seemed as though every feeling of his soul breathed purity, righteousness, and love; hence he was at all times able to bear a strong testimony against all impurity, unrighteousness, and every kind of evil. He often said, "The Gospel is without fault; it is as straight as straightness; it is pure as the heavens; and if you do not obey it, you will lose your souls."

12. With tears rolling from his eyes, he frequently expressed his love to God, and his thankfulness for the Gospel, in the following language: "O how precious is the way of God to my thirsty soul! I feel the love of God continually flowing into my soul, like rivers of living water! It is sweeter to my taste than honey in the honey-comb!

I know that God owns me for his son, and yet I will pray to Him. I know how to pray, and I know how to be thankful for the Gospel. Even my breath is continual prayer to God."

13. He used to say: "I could willingly lay down my life for my brethren, if I were called to it; for I feel that degree of love for them, that they are near and dear to me like my own soul. My only treasure upon earth is in them that believe. I have no relation except in the people of God. They who are faithful to serve God are my relations; they are my interest and my treasure, and all I have is theirs."

14. Some individuals, who had great faith in Mother Ann, and were zealous during her ministration, suffered great loss after she was taken from them; for their faith centred in her person, and not in the revelation and power of God which dwelt in her, and which was transmitted through her to her successors. Father James felt a deep sense of their danger from this source; and being impressed with the unspeakable worth of souls, and the great importance of a deep and genuine work

of salvation in every soul, he did not cease to warn the people, with many tears, to be faithful and persevering, so as not to lose that which they had already gained, by neglecting to labor for an increase of the Gospel in their own souls.

15. In solemn warnings to the people, and for their encouragement, he used to say: "Wherever you are, whatever may betide you, how dark soever things may appear, how unjustly soever you may suffer, keep your faith; for the time will come when all wrongs will be righted, and every one will receive a just reward. I am not ashamed to build up your faith; for your faith is most holy. But I know you have infirmities, and I pray that the forbearance of God may be lengthened out to you, till you learn to do right; for you must have an exceeding righteousness; your righteousness must exceed the righteousness of the scribes and pharisees. Therefore, preserve within your hearts that holy treasure which will keep you in time of trouble. Keep your faith; for the end of your faith will be the salvation of your souls. When I am gone, and you see the branches grow and flourish, then

know ye that the root is holy. I have ventured my life and soul among you, and you have received the Gospel, and you are welcome to it."

16 Father James, in seasons of Divine worship, often publicly abased himself before God, in deep humiliation of soul. One Sabbath day, at Harvard, he addressed a large concourse of persons with great solemnity, and evidently under a great weight of the power of God, which brought a very solemn and affecting sensation upon the whole assembly. He then knelt down, and the Believers immediately fell upon their knees, and many other persons, who were deeply affected with his discourse, did the same. While thus on his knees, in profound humiliation, he uttered these words: "I am but a poor worm of the dust, and a very little one, too. I feel oftentimes as though I could crumble into the dust before God." He often abased himself in this manner.

17. At another time, in a public assembly, at Enfield, before he began to speak, he knelt down, and, in tribulation of spirit, said: "God has committed the Gospel to my trust." He paused,

while the tears flowed plentifully down his cheeks. He then proceeded: "I pray that God would lay nothing to my charge. Christ is revealed. I feel his power in sorrow and in love. God has blessed me with a broken heart and godly sorrow for sin." After this he delivered a very affecting discourse, in which he preached the Gospel of self-denial and the cross, and urged the absolute necessity of confessing and forsaking all sin, and concluded in these words: "As you treat this Gospel, so God will treat you. If you slight it, God will slight you; if you regard it, God will regard you. For, as the testimony of Noah condemned the old world, so shall this testimony condemn the present generation."

18. Father James often solemnly warned Believers not to suffer themselves to be overshadowed and darkened with those things which have a tendency to shut the gift of God from the soul. "I warn you, brethren," said he, "not to be overcome with the cares of this world, lest your souls lose the power of God, and you become lean and barren." "The way to labor for the Gospel is to

keep your minds exercised in laboring upon the things that belong to your peace, and not on the things of the world; for if you give your minds to labor upon the things of the world, they will become corrupted." "You ought to be watchful over your words at all times, and be careful to know that you speak the truth; and not tell things you do not know to be true, in such a manner as to deceive others. You ought to represent things as they are, and not deceive one another: it is lying; it is wicked."

19. He used often to say: "Be what you seem to be, and seem to be what you really are. Don't carry two faces. You that dare use deceit, remember what I say: God will yet meet you in a strait place." In reproving Believers, he used to say: "If you don't love to hear of these things, then leave them off. Put away the cause, and the effect will cease. I will know no man by his speech, but by the fruit he brings forth. Ye who have believed in God, be careful to maintain good works."

20. In the time of Shay's insurrection in Mas-

sachusetts, some of the Believers, in expressing their sentiments, manifested some party feelings concerning that event; but Father James rebuked that spirit, and said: "They who give way to a party spirit, and are influenced by the divisions and contentions of the world, so as to feel for one political party more than for another, have no part with me. The spirit of party is the spirit of the world; and whoever indulges in it, and unites with one evil spirit against another, is off from Christian ground."

21. In addressing a public assembly of Believers at Ashfield, he said: "You ought to fear God in all you do. When you are about your work, you ought to fear God. And even in the gifts of God, and under the operations of the power of God, you ought to keep the fear of God, lest, by feeling releasement in those gifts, you run into lightness. There are many pious souls in this world, who live up to the best light they know, that have never heard the sound of this Gospel; but, except your righteousness shall exceed theirs, you will in nowise enter into the kingdom of heaven. Heaven

is a place of joy and tranquillity to those who find it. But I am jealous, and with a godly jealousy, too, that there are some here that never will find it." He further said: "Those who are called by the Gospel when they are children, and are faithful and obedient, and keep out of sin, will be the flower of heaven and the glory of paradise."

22. One Sabbath day, at Harvard, when the Believers were assembled together for worship, and were all sitting in profound silence, Father James, under a solemn weight of the power of God, suddenly raised both his hands, and exclaimed: "Heavens! heavens! heavens!" and instantly the house was shaken, and the casements clattered, as though the house had been shaken by a mighty earthquake. At another time, under a similar spiritual impression, he uttered the words, "Peace! peace! peace! What peace I feel! The peace of the Gospel is worth more than all the treasures of this world."

23. One day he was speaking respecting the privilege and call of Believers to rise out of the generative order, with all its animal, selfish ties

and relations, and he said: "I hate these things, as I hate the smoke of the bottomless pit. And, in lieu thereof, I behold in open vision the angelic hosts, and join in their melodious songs of praise and adoration."

24. One evening, in meeting, he said: "I should be glad to speak a few words, though I would not speak anything that is too hard for you to understand.

25. "I believe I was six hours, last night, in the belly of hell! Indeed, I know I was; and I preached to the spirits in prison. I never knew until then what that passage of Scripture signifies, which says, 'One day with the Lord is as a thousand years, and a thousand years as one day.' But now, by what I have seen and felt, I can testify that, to a soul that has been in hell but *one day*, it appears like a thousand years. For the horrors of souls in hell are so extreme, and their banishment from God so great, that they can not measure time. It is called the bottomless pit, and souls in it feel themselves sinking further and further from God; and what still increases their tor-

ment is, they can see no way out. If a man should live to the age of Methuselah, and go through all the miseries of this life, it could not be compared to one day in hell. When I saw the state of the damned, I shuddered at the awful prospect.

26. "If you will take up your crosses against the work of generation, and will follow Christ Jesus in the regeneration, God will cleanse you from all unrighteousness. Men and women in this world can please themselves by fleshly gratifications; and, if they do not overcome their passions by the Gospel, they carry them with them into the world of spirits. Death does not destroy those passions, nor make them less powerful. But souls in hell feel their lustful passions rise a thousand times stronger in them than when in this world; yet they can find no way by which to gratify them; therefore their lust is their torment, and it torments them in proportion to its rage. They also feel the wrath of God against that filthy nature, and this is still a greater torment to them.

27. "I see, in open vision, souls in hell, under torment for their sins, which (were they in the

body) would be enough to take away their natural lives.

28. "Souls that go out of this world, who have not heard the Gospel, do not know God, nor where to find Him. I have seen them wandering about, trying to find God, weeping and crying until, to appearance, they had worn gutters in their cheeks. All souls will be judged by the testimony of the Gospel, which you now hear."

29. About the middle of January, 1787, Father James, having assembled the Believers in New Lebanon together in the meeting-house, came in under great heaviness of spirit, and, with tears flowing copiously, said: "I am going to leave you. I feel that my work is done here, and I do not know that I shall ever see you again in this world; but I leave those with you who are able to teach you the way of God. I desire that you would treasure up the Gospel, and make it your only interest. You are all the interest I have in this world. I have no other interest."

30. He then knelt down, and wept exceedingly. All the assembly knelt with him. After rising, he

warned the people, in a very feeling and affecting address, to be faithful, and keep the way of God, when he was gone, saying: "We have given you the Gospel; see to it that you make a good use of it. Do abide faithful. Those of you who abide faithful will be like a bud in the bloom; but those who do not abide will be like a falling leaf; and you will remember these words when you can not see me."

31. He then addressed the elders and laborers among the people, and gave them a very solemn charge to be faithful and watch over the people for their protection. Said he: "Deal with the brethren and sisters as I have dealt with you." He also warned them in a very special manner concerning the youth and children, saying: "You must take care of the rising generation; for, if they are protected, the time will come when they will be the flower of the people of God."

32. The next morning, he set off for Enfield, in Connecticut, from whence he never returned. After tarrying a short time there, he visited the Believers at Harvard, Shirley, Woburn, and other

places, where they then resided, and returned to Enfield in March, where he remained, and was continually visited by Believers till his decease.

33. Father James's ministry was short, but very active and laborious. He visited all the different places in the land where the Gospel had been planted—some of them several times. His labors were continually employed in strengthening the weak, comforting the afflicted, and purging out sin. It was the peculiar gift of his ministry to wean the affections of Believers from their natural and earthly ties, and prepare them for a spiritual relation in Church order, which he foretold was at hand, and often spoke of it. His instructions to Elder Joseph Meacham and those with him, relative to gathering, building, and establishing the Church in Gospel order, might with great propriety be likened to the instructions of David to Solomon, concerning the building of the temple, which was an eminent type of this very work.

34. Many were the instructions, exhortations, and solemn warnings that Father James delivered in the last days of his ministry. When he came

near the close of his life he said: "I have given you my life; all I have I have given to you. If I ever had anything, you possess it—it is yours; now see that you make a good use of it." About a fortnight before his decease, he said: "My body is under great sufferings, but I feel my soul at peace with God and man. I have given you the Gospel; now see to it what kind of use you make of it. If you keep the Gospel, the Gospel will keep you. I have given my life for the people. After I am gone there will be a great increase."

35. A little before his decease, a number of brethren and sisters came from New Lebanon to see him; and, when about to return home, they went into his room to take their leave of him. On entering his room, they all knelt down in sorrow and tears, and in prayer to God, feeling sensible that this would be the last time they should see him in this world. He addressed them as follows: "I feel thankful to see you all, and that you have come to see me in my sickness once more, before I leave the world. I feel weak in body, but comfortable in my spirit; and, whether I live or die, the

Gospel will increase. I have had a great desire to come and see you all, but I have not been able. But my heart has been with you; and now your hearts must be with me, to labor for the power of God—for *one union*. I desire you would give my love to the people where you go, and tell them that I am alive, and that I never expect to die; for the sting of death is taken from me, and all fear and terror; yet I expect soon to put off this earthly tabernacle. Farewell."

36. When he was dying, a number of the brethren and sisters went to see him. On inquiring how he felt, he said: "My sufferings are exceedingly great; but that peace and consolation that I feel in the Gospel I would not exchange for a thousand such worlds as this." He then exhorted all to hold on, and to hold out to the end, and said: "If you hold out to the end, you will feel that peace which I feel."

37. Thus he continued to exhort, strengthen, and encourage all around him till he expired, July 20th, 1787, in the 37th year of his age. His funeral was attended on the following day. The

scene was very affecting to all the Believers, who viewed him as their Elder and Father, and the last of those faithful ministers of Christ who brought the Gospel of salvation to this land, and who had been called to stand in the Ministry.

CHAPTER XIV.

JOHN HOCKNELL.

1. John Hocknell was a native of Cheshire, in England, a man of respectable character, and possessed considerable property. He formerly belonged to the Methodist Society, but afterwards he became a zealous member of the Society under Jane and James Wardley, and readily embraced the increasing light through Mother Ann, and became a faithful Believer.

2. He was a man of very meek deportment, and was greatly gifted in visions and prophecies; he also possessed the gift of healing. He was a great help to Mother Ann and her little family, in a temporal view, and was very zealous in the support of the Gospel. It was through his instrumentality that they were enabled to cross the ocean, and

establish themselves in this land. Indeed, the temporal assistance which his zeal and liberality afforded the Society, in its infant state, was its principal dependence. He was a very honest, conscientious, and upright man, and continued faithful and zealous during life. He saw the Church established in Gospel order, and with great joy saw its growing prosperity in things temporal and spiritual. He departed this life Feb. 27, 1799, aged 76 years.

CHAPTER XV.

JOSEPH MEACHAM AND LUCY WRIGHT.

1. JOSEPH MEACHAM and LUCY WRIGHT were among the first of those in America who received faith in the religious principles of Shakerism. Upon them the leadership and government of the people (Shakers) devolved. Under their administration it was that the principles in regard to property and order in general were fully carried out and established.

2. They gradually gathered the people from their scattered condition into families, having their property in common. Orders, rules, and regulations, in temporal and spiritual things, were framed, appropriate to the new relations they were then coming into as a body of people. Elders and deacons of both sexes were appointed, and set in

their proper order; and a Covenant was written and entered into for the mutual understanding and protection of the members.

3. The Society at New Lebanon was the first that was organized, and is the center of union to all the other societies. Yet the immediate duties of the Ministry (who are the Elders of the elders) extend only to the two societies of New Lebanon and Watervliet. The other societies are under the direction of Ministries appointed to preside over them. In most instances, two or three societies constitute a bishopric, being united under the superintendence of the same Ministry.

4. Joseph Meacham was born at Enfield, Conn., on the 22d of February, 1742, and deceased on the 16th of August, 1796.

5. Lucy Wright succeeded Joseph Meacham in the lead of the Society. During her administration, the several societies in the States of Ohio and Kentucky were established, and large accessions were made to the Eastern societies.

6. She was born in Pittsfield, Mass., February 5th, 1760, and deceased February 7th, 1821.

7. The wife and family of JOSEPH MEACHAM were gathered with him into the Society. He had been a minister or elder of the *Baptist* denomination, in which he was highly esteemed for his private virtues, as an exemplary and pious professor, and as an able, efficient teacher. He was also distinguished among his clerical brethren, on account of his superior natural and acquired abilities; he being of a sound, philosophical and practical turn of mind, yet spiritual to such an extent as to be looked up to, by all his religious associates, as the right man to direct the great revival; for he was the master spirit in the movement of the spiritual elements that occured in New Lebanon and vicinity preceding the going forth of the Gospel testimony. And for no one thing was he more esteemed and reverenced by his peers, than for his superior wisdom and discretion—a *right use* of the scientific and spiritual knowledge with which he was endowed.

8. It is also considered, by Believers, that his gift of Divine revelation was deeper than that of any other person, excepting *Mother Ann.*

9. Many of the peculiar *devotional* exercises of the Shakers were brought by him from the spirit world. In the same way he also laid the foundation of the *temporal* economy of Believers.

10. The true relation of man to the *animal* creation was also, by this means, fully established among Believers; and, while all neglect, or abuse, of any animal, on the one hand, was utterly prohibited; so, on the other, all idolizing, or undue familiarity, with any dumb beast was equally discountenanced, particularly the cat, the dog, and the horse.

11. *Spiritualism* itself is not yet sufficiently advanced, to bear the relation of some incidents that occurred in the latter part of the experience of *Joseph Meacham*, exhibiting the power which mankind, as lords and rulers of earth, will possess over the inferior orders of sentient creatures, when themselves shall be redeemed to, and stand in, the Divine order.

12. LUCY WRIGHT, who (with her husband) united with the society at the age of twenty-one, was a true counterpart of, and fit companion for *Father Joseph*, in gathering Believers into Church order. She was of one of the most respectable families in Pittsfield, and was possessed of a high order of native talent and intellectuality, and a refined education, conjoined to a solid religious experience, and a pure devotional spirit; all of which combined, fitted her for becoming the external leader, and a spiritual mother of the new creation into which God had so providentially called her.

Under their administration, some of the noblest, intellectual and spiritually-minded men and women that the country at that time possessed, were gathered to the Gospel; and the societies of Shakers which by those persons were founded in various parts of the United States, bear witness to their ability, and their zeal and devotedness to truth, as also to the knowledge and wisdom by which that zeal was directed. These were "kings and priests unto God" and man— "the light of the world"—"the salt of the earth;" and the blessing of unborn generations will, like the gentle dews of heaven, rest upon their memories, for the self-sacrificing and unselfish consecration of their "*all*" to that Gospel which will yet, to the spiritually religious part of our race, be what the gold mines of California and Australia have proved to the restless, physical generative man—even "the pearl of great price;" so great, that, like Father Joseph and Mother Lucy, they will "sell all," and "forsake all" other ties and relations, to obtain it; and, like them, will many of the *true* kings and queens of the earth bow themselves down to the yoke of the Gospel, that they may "win Christ," and attain to the power of his resurrection.

NOTE.—For further and fuller particulars of the history, doctrines, laws, orders, etc., of the Society and its Founders, the reader is referred to the works published by the United Society, but more especially to the one entitled "*Christ's First and Second Appearing,*" and to another entitled "*A Summary View of the Millennial Church,*" which can be had on application to any of the societies.

STANDARD WORKS

PUBLISHED BY THE

United Society of Believers, called Shakers

The Testimony of Christ's Second Appearing, exemplified by the Principles and Practice of the true Church of Christ.—History of the Progressive Work of God, extending from the Creation of Man to the "Harvest," comprising the Four Great Dispensations now consummating in the Millennial Church.—Antichrist's Kingdom, or Churches, contrasted with the Church of Christ's Second Appearing, the Kingdom of the God of Heaven. By BENJAMIN YOUNGS and CALVIN GREEN. Medium 8vo; pp. 650. Price $1 25

The Manifesto; or, a Declaration of the Doctrines and Practice of the Church of Christ. By JOHN DUNLAVY. Medium 8vo; pp. 486. Price $1

A Summary View of the Millennial Church; or, United Society of Believers, comprising the Rise, Progress, and Practical Order of the Society; together with the general Principles of their Faith and Testimony. By CALVIN GREEN. Medium 12mo; pp. 384. Price 50 cents

Tests of Divine Inspiration; or, the Rudimental Principles by which True and False Revelation, in all Eras of the

World, can be uniformly discriminated. By F. W. EVANS. Pamphlet; medium 12mo; pp. 126. Price 18 cents.

Three Discourses:—On the Order and Propriety of Divine Inspiration and Revelation, showing the Necessity thereof, in all Ages, to know the Will of God;—On the Second Appearing of Christ in the Order of the Female;—and On a United Inheritance in all Things, in order to support a true Christian Community. By WM. LEONARD. Pamphlet; medium 12mo; pp. 88. Price One Shilling.

Brief Exposition of the Established Principles and Regulations of the United Society of Believers. By CALVIN GREEN. Pamphlet; medium 12mo; pp. 38. Price 6 cents.

A Short Treatise on the Second Appearing of Christ, in and through the Order of the Female. By F. W. EVANS. Pamphlet; medium 12mo; pp. 24. Price 6 cents.

Plain Evidences, by which the True Church of Christ may be known and distinguished from all others. Extracted from the "Manifesto." Pamphlet; medium 12mo; pp 120. Price One Shilling.